THE
DEATH
OF ART

THE
DEATH
OF ART

*Black and White
in the Recent Southern Novel*

FLOYD C. WATKINS

*MERCER UNIVERSITY LAMAR
MEMORIAL LECTURES, NO. 13*

UNIVERSITY OF GEORGIA PRESS

ATHENS

For Anna

Contents

I RACISM IN FICTION 1

II THE BLACK 11

III THE WHITE 35

IV ALIENATED NOVELISTS 61

NOTES 67

BIBLIOGRAPHY 71

INDEX 75

Preface

MODERN SOUTHERN NOVELS WHICH TREAT THE RELATIONSHIP between the black man and the white man are highly prejudiced against the white. It may be possible to defend this bias as a historical, political, and social corrective; but as fiction the bias fails. Such is the thesis of this book.

These lectures were delivered at Mercer University on November 13 and 14, 1969. Mercer and Macon have preserved a friendliness and sense of community which made happy the visit of my wife and me. Professors Ben W. Griffith and Spencer B. King were especially kind.

In my research I have benefited from the wise counsel and the good advice of Frank Manley and William B. Dillingham, who have read the manuscript and helped me to wrestle with the difficulties. The staff of the Emory University Library, and especially Miss Joyce Werner, have helped me in fundamental research. Richard L. Hall did much of the preliminary bibliographical work. Emory University generously gave me two quarters of time to read novels and meditate.

FLOYD C. WATKINS

Emory University
Atlanta, Georgia

Protest qua protest denies the textures of life. The problem is to permit the fullest range of life into racial awareness.

—Robert Penn Warren, *Writers at Work*

ONE

Racism in Fiction

IT MAY BE IMPOSSIBLE TO WRITE A GOOD NOVEL ABOUT THE race question. Art treats the human condition. An author must not permit controversy or doctrine to dictate his opinions and his treatment of his characters. The poet, Allen Tate believes, "has a great responsibility . . . to write poems, and not to gad about using the rumor of his verse . . . as the excuse to appear on platforms and to view with alarm."[1] Similarly, a Southern novelist must not use his fiction as a vehicle for propaganda about the relationship between white and black. The novelist who labors to make the relationship between the races his main subject may have an interest which overrides his desire to write fiction. Is William Faulkner's *Absalom, Absalom!* primarily about the white's relationship to the Negro? No. But it may be as much about this topic as any good novel can be.

The best literature does not thrive in an atmosphere of angry contention. Most men of letters in the early South were political; they felt obligated to join in the furious struggles against first Great Britain and then the North. Those who did write poetry or fiction were mainly gentleman amateurs. The best Southern literature was written in a few decades after World War I, but the Southern Renaissance now seems to be ending. The troublesome issues of our time may be in part responsible for the decline. It has been more than fifteen years now since the

Supreme Court made its decision to end racial segregation in schools. Since then a social revolution has begun with race as the issue, and Southern white novelists have become deeply involved in the controversies. I do not know how many novels they have written about the problems of race, but recently I have read approximately forty that deal with the subject in some way.[2] The Southern writer is again dedicating his efforts to political issues, but now he is working mainly within his art, or trying to, rather than giving himself unabashedly to political and social questions. In Allen Tate's term these writers are "sociologists of fiction."[3]

The two most harassed peoples in America in many ways are Negroes and Southern whites. Perhaps it is human nature that for more than a century they have let the Northerner and the outsider set them at each other's throats. Both peoples are minorities, even though in extremely different ways. They share a great deal in culture, in hardships, and in virtues. "If the writer exists for any social good," according to Ralph Ellison, "his role is that of preserving in art those human values which can endure by confronting change. . . . I speak of the faith, the patience, the humor, the sense of timing, rugged sense of life and the manner of expressing it which all go to define the American Negro."[4] These virtues are almost as true of one race as they are of another. But Southern novels have given these human values racial tags in recent times: except in a few instances, Negroes have the humane values, and whites do not. Race distinguishes the good guys and the bad almost as accurately as the white and black hats did in old Western movies. In the hands of the Southern white author the novel has become a weapon turned against his own race.

Good regional literature treats the spirit of man as a subject and uses local customs and trappings to furnish poetic particulars. When the localism becomes more significant than the individuality of the characters, then the author is not looking to his first task. A local color writer like Mary Noailles Murfree never created a character with full dignity and depth. In contrast, Faulkner revealed much human complexity in backward Southerners like the Bundren family in *As I Lay Dying*. Since 1954 Southern novels written about race often exhibit some of the flaws and oversimplifications in the local color writing of the nineteenth century; but instead of treating the goodness of all minorities, most fiction idealizes the Negro and condemns the white. These novels are untrue to the facts of Southern life and, more important, untrue to the spirit of man.

One of the least bigoted of these novels is Mary Fassett Hunt's *Joanna Lord*. But it is first, foremost, and always a novel about the South. That is its artistic failure. Its theme is Southern, political, racial—not adequately human. Although Mrs. Hunt has created the most admirable segregationist found in any modern fiction, her novel contains many stereotypes. On the other hand, Reynolds Price's *A Long and Happy Life* may stand or fall as a novel rather than a tract. It has important Negro characters, but its subject is not the good Negro and the bad white. It does not divide its characters into Negroes and Negro-lovers and Negro-haters. Such simple classifications as this reflect the main flaw of the novel of propaganda. Hugh Park has written a column about three Negro nurses in "spotless white uniforms" waiting on an expressway in hot weather for someone to stop and help them change a flat tire. After "hundreds of cars" passed them by, a "well-dressed man" stopped, jacked up the car, and changed the tire. "He was white, had an Alabama license (Montgomery) and a Wallace sticker on his bumper."[5]

In most recent Southern novels segregationists are incapable of such human kindness. Color determines virtue. White characters represent racial and moral principles; they do not live moral-immoral lives like the protagonists in novels by authors like Graham Greene and Robert Penn Warren. Great literature creates man as a creature "of opposites, of good and evil, of instinct and intellect, of passion and spirituality."[6] A man who is not a creature of opposites is a poor subject for literature, and novels written about such an abnormal creature must themselves be poor. If Southern whites are as bad as white novelists have made them out to be in the last fifteen years, they are too simple to be worthy characters. A political and a moral line which follows a color line is absurd, and that exact kind of absurdity pervades the newest Southern fiction. If great novels about relationships between white and black are ever to be created, they will have to be written by novelists profoundly aware of all emotional reactions to race and yet detached enough personally to be objective.

From the first, Negro critics have complained about the portraits of the black man in American literature. "It is unfortunate for the Negro," Ralph Ellison has written, "that the most powerful formulations of modern American fictional works have been so slanted against him that when he approaches for a glimpse of himself he discovers an image drained of humanity."[7] Sterling A. Brown argues that it is "obviously dangerous . . . to rely upon literary artists when they advance themselves as sociologists and ethnologists."[8] In the 1930s Brown objected most to stereotypes, like the comic Negro, the brute Negro, the tragic mulatto. "Any stereotyping is fatal to great, or even to convincing literature" (p. 180). Even if a stereotype exists in the flesh, it does not make convincing fiction. "The Negro stereotype" in American literature, Ellison writes, "is really an image of the unorganized, irrational forces of American life."[9] Strangely, a Negro talking about the Negro has here precisely described the white character in contemporary Southern fiction. The white has been "drained of humanity" as the Negro used to be. A strange welter of forces has caused the white novelist to repudiate white people and to deal with them in such terms as to suggest that he knows nothing at all about them.

Ben Haas's *Look Away, Look Away* typically treats the life of a nonviolent Negro saint, a leader in disposition and stature comparable to Martin Luther King. At the end of the book the untainted hero walks toward rabid whites who have killed his wife and who will probably assassinate him. I finished the novel on the morning of April 4, 1968. Before I heard the news of Dr. King's murder, I was convinced that Haas's book was an oversimplification. After I heard of Dr. King's death, I could not regard *Look Away, Look Away* as anything but a bad novel even though such tragic events as it describes do happen. Art demands complexity which may not be revealed in journalistic skeletal outlines. *Look Away, Look Away* oversimplifies, treats people as social issues, creates stereotypes, equates morality with race and political views, exaggerates sensationalism and melodrama. Fiction can be extreme and untrue even when it is based on reality and when it prophesies coming violence.

Great literature is not easily predictable. When a similar cast of characters is repeated in many novels, obviously something other than the imaginations of good writers is in control. In recent Southern fiction which treats the race question, the same types of personae appear over and over. Characters fall into patterns designed to convey social messages. Generally a small segment of the white society aligns itself with the cause of racial harmony or integration. The most constantly recurring character is the solitary good white man. He is moral, loving, kind, gentle—never evil or obnoxious or even bad-tempered. Character corresponds exactly with views of race. No character like Ben-

jamin F. "Beast" Butler of Reconstruction times helps
the cause of civil rights for his own selfish reasons. Only one
or two good white persons live in most of these fictitious
communities. Only Harper Lee's *To Kill a Mockingbird*
portrays more than a half dozen good white persons in the
community, and even here only a "handful of people in
this town say that fair play is not marked White Only. . ."
(p. 249).

Homelessness or an unsatisfactory marriage is often the
lot of the good liberal white character. For some reason
only one of about two dozen marriages is portrayed at
length as happy wedlock between two Southerners.[10] A few
other marriages between Southerners are fairly harmonious. Southerners who have married wives not from the
South are almost always ecstatically happy. One of the most
blissful marriages occurs in one of the most anti-white
novels of all, Jesse Hill Ford's *The Liberation of Lord
Byron Jones.* This happy couple are the only white persons
of liberal tendencies in the book. Three good white protagonists are bachelors; one is an unmarried female teacher; five are widows or widowers; two are unhappily married
to Southern white women. Does the author's interest in
race control his portrait of the marriages of his characters?
Probably. When the liberal hero lacks happiness in love
and marriage, the novelist slyly suggests that he is paying
for the racial sins of his regional compatriots. The evils of
the South symbolically isolate anyone who is kind to the
black man, or tolerant of him.

Almost all the imperfections and flaws of even the good
whites are in some way connected to a failure to believe or
do the right thing about race. An aristocrat helps a black
boy to become a physician in Mary Beechwood's *Memphis
Jackson's Son,* but even this racial philanthropist patronizes
the Negro: "It was amazing, he thought, how kind, how
downright decent some of them were under their black

hides" (p. 143). The surprise at goodness indicates contempt for the race and the character of the Negro. War or
death, the same man seems to think, should follow racial
patterns, should take the life of the black man before the
white. This white man is bitter that he has lost his son, "a
handsome spirited lad," and that "a stumbling black boy"
is left "in his place" (p. 143).

Moderates have always maintained that a very small minority causes the evils in relationships between races. The
father of a child who attempts to integrate a Southern
school in Douglas Kiker's *The Southerner* reminds his
white friend that "ninety-nine percent of the people in the
South are good people, Jess, but they do things they don't
really want to do. They are ashamed of themselves for it"
(p. 242). But the novelists pay only abstract lip service to
the existence of such Southerners; indeed, few besides
Kiker even assert that such a majority of good people exists; and Kiker, like the rest, creates far more bad Southerners than good ones. Only one Southern white in his novel
has the courage to tell the truth in a trial. One son of a
cotton mill owner prevents a white mob and black mob
from clashing, but this courageous man advises his friend
not to antagonize whites by testifying in the trial of a Negro. Toward the end of the novel Kiker has his hero re-
nounce all Southerners because a small percentage are evil:
"The irreconcilable part of it was that, in repudiating the
evil in the South, you also had to repudiate the good, the
good people—and the great majority of Southerners were
good people—and the good things about the place—the
loyalty of friendship, the charity, the honor. But you could
not reject a part without rejecting the whole because, God
help us, we were all bound together in this thing" (p. 294).
The people in Elliott Chaze's *Tiger in the Honeysuckle*
would be as friendly as any people on earth "If you sub-
tracted the racial situation. . . . But, of course, you couldn't

subtract it. The disease was in terminal stage, inoperable"
(p. 248).

So the novelist and his hero usually reject the entire
Southern tradition. In William Hoffman's *The Trumpet
Unblown,* for example, a group of violent low-class Southerners are called the Kentuckians over and over as the
novelist emphasizes his social generalization. The protagonist, an aristocratic Virginian, is unable to endure the
trials of World War II. He contracts a venereal disease and
suffers from alcoholism and delirium tremens. Psychologi-
cally and morally broken, he says that the "ideal and fancy
sentiments" of his old Richmond family "just won't work
any longer" (p. 289). He finds nothing to replace his tradition, but he "would have gladly taken up their values again
if all it involved was putting them on like a hat" (p. 297).

The good Southerner is always subject to an abrupt fall.
Or possibly some guilt-ridden novelists have difficulty al-
lowing even one character to be consistently kind to Negroes. In William Styron's *Set This House on Fire* the
main character, Cass, cannot rid himself of a feeling of
guilt about the Negro. "There was always a nigger in the
woodpile somewhere, and you'd have thought that as a nice
southern boy who was maybe just a little brighter than
some of my cornfield brethren I'd have had it all doped out
a little bit sooner" (p. 369). Cass accompanies a Negro-
hater named Lonnie when he goes to repossess a radio. The
Negro family is not at home. When Lonnie enters the
house and finds that the radio has been cracked, he goes
into a "frantic . . . rage and frustration and unstoppered
resentment" (p. 376). He reduces the interior of the Negro
home to rubbish. Cass, good as he is, shares this "maniac's
fury" and becomes "set on teaching the niggers, too." He
helps turn over the stove. The feeling was in his "loins, hot,
flowing, sexual." If this scene is well motivated (and I don't

think it is), no white Southerner can ever trust his constancy in his attitude toward the black man.

In *To Kill a Mockingbird* Harper Lee does attempt to create a complex segregationist. The newspaper editor Braxton Underwood "despises Negroes, won't have one near him" (p. 167). But when a mob threatens to take the noble Negro Tom from jail and to lynch him, Mr. Underwood keeps Atticus covered with a double-barreled shotgun to protect him until the mob leaves. Here Miss Lee attempts to introduce moral complexity, but the editor makes such a brief and superficial appearance that the scene appears merely sentimental. The opposing forces within him are shown in only one simple event, and the action he takes works only for good. There are numerous good characters in Faulkner's *The Reivers*, but the novel is not primarily about race as so many others are, and it is as sentimental about good whites as it is about good Negroes. Robert Penn Warren in *Flood* does not regard goodness and blackness as synonymous, but he does follow the pattern of race novels in regard to education. An intellectual lawyer who is the most liberal-minded citizen of the town on the subject of race has a Negro mistress. He can find a man of mind only among the Negroes. He tells a Negro minister, "I don't have anybody to talk to except when you come, and by then, I'm ready to blow the gasket" (p. 296).

The damage to Southern fiction resulting from such one-sidedness is tremendous. The heroes struggle against the world, but they see the truth so completely and ideally that the profound struggle that exists within a great character in fiction seldom enters these novels. The hero's beliefs are pre-established, and he never has to fight his way through to a new clarity of vision and understanding. The struggles are external against a world of fanatical extremists, and action becomes about as important as a chase by a posse in a Western motion picture. And the issues are just about as superficial and clear-cut as when the ugly land-hungry villain tries to foreclose the mortgage on the beautiful and helpless damsel who has inherited her father's ranch.

TWO

The Black

WHITE AUTHORS OF RACIST FICTION OFTEN WORK THEM-
selves into a position which is morally and philosophically
inconsistent and illogical: good in the Negro comes from
the Negro himself acting in full freedom of the will; bad
in the Negro is sociologically determined and is attributa-
ble to the evils caused by a white society. The black man is
responsible for his goodness, not responsible for his evil.
The white, on the other hand, generally has much more
freedom of the will than the Negro, even in the same novel.
Evil whites predominate, and they are morally responsible
for their choices. All the devices of determinism, natural-
ism, environmental control, and psychology are turned
against the society that prevents the Negro's realization of
himself. Novelists permit their attitudes toward race to
dictate their beliefs about man.

Society, of course, does determine much of the Negro's
way of life in America: any man's life is in part determined
and controlled. The critic, the artist, and the social scien-
tist all agree that Southern society has controlled "the ways
by which . . . Negroes confronted their destiny"[1] and that
"certain psychological attitudes [are] brought to Negro
life by whites."[2] But no person of good mind can accept the
practice of the numerous novelists who assume that the
goodness of the Negro springs from within and who explain
Negro crime and immorality as something coming entirely
from outside. If Ellison is correct in saying that "it is almost

impossible for many whites to consider questions of sex, women, economic opportunity, the national identity, historic change, social justice . . . without summoning malignant images of black men into consciousness,"[3] white novelists are certainly exceptions to the rule. They summon "malignant images" of white men into consciousness and benevolent images of black men. Socially they attempt to overcompensate for the past, but no artist can write great fiction when he begins with a predetermined and controlling social purpose.

The Negro revolution has come because the Negro has not thought that he was receiving his "human rating."[4] "What you'd have the world accept as *me*," the Negro would say to the novelist, "isn't even human."[5] But since 1954, at least, the Southern white could make the same statement about fiction; and he could complain not only about stereotypes but also about the description of his morality. Perhaps the Negro should still protest, but now his reasons would be altogether different. He "isn't even human" now because he is depicted as too good to be true. For decades Negroes played subservient roles in television if they appeared at all. The comic sidekick like Rochester on Jack Benny's program is a thing of the past, and Negroes who are in spy or crime serials on television usually dominate their white cohorts in character, personality, and intelligence.

The Negro is justified in demanding to be accepted as a man. But that acceptance means that he must also admit his flaws and that novelists must depict them. Robert Penn Warren says that "the notion that the Negro—*qua* Negro—is intrinsically 'better' " is sentimentality.

> This betterness is described in many forms, but, strangely enough, you never hear *the* Negro admired as a better philosopher, mathematician, nuclear physicist, banker, soldier, lawyer, or administrator. It would seem that the

betterness is always something that can be attributed to the Noble Savage—if we give a rather generous interpretation to that term. This modern American Noble Savage is admired for athletic prowess, musicality, grace in the dance, heroic virtue, natural humor, tenderness with children, patience, sensitivity to nature, generosity of spirit, capacity to forgive, life awareness, and innocent sexuality.[6]

The Negro, according to Warren, resents this kind of praise, and Negro critics consequently often dislike fiction which draws favorable portraits of Negroes. The Negro resents the condescension of the white novelist who recognizes "simple worth" in black characters.[7] A Negro librarian told me that no white man since 1954 has written a good novel about the Negro. Perhaps no white man can write a good novel about the Negro *race*, certainly not with this kind of praise.

Out of guilt, especially since 1954, the white novelist has turned the Southern "fear of what is mysteriously different" into its "inevitably linked opposite, an attraction; loathing becomes desire, strangely mixed." That "desire" resembles what some elements in the South have always termed "nigger-loving." It should be objectionable to both white and black because it loves the individual man only as a member of a race, not for himself. A good novelist cannot allow himself to love Negroes more than whites, especially for the wrong reasons. To the white novelist the Negro is, among other things, what Warren calls "the Noble Savage. He becomes the symbolic vessel of a number of things we yearn for, the image in which we find our vicarious satisfactions. And this modern American Noble Savage is obtruded upon the scene at a moment when the tensions of civilization are unusually high. . . . There is no wonder," Warren continues, "that to many the Noble Savage appears as a redeemer."[8] But what does the Negro redeem the white from? Mainly his excessive guilt over the sins of his ancestors. The white novelist's image of the Negro as Noble Savage makes him use the Negro as earlier Americans wrote about the frontiersman. He turns to the Negro in an attempt to escape his own unathletic, urban, unnatural, asexual, phony world. By comparison, the black world may seem fundamental and unspoiled. The Negro is an escape to Noble Savagery, and again the individual is not recognized as a man with both faults and virtues. The result is a fiction of freaks: freak clothes, freak violence, freak goodness, freak people. Art is destroyed when the illusion of humanity is diminished. A certain core of normalcy is necessary if the characters are to be human at all.

Even well-known novels like Carson McCullers' *Clock Without Hands,* William Faulkner's *The Reivers,* and Harper Lee's *To Kill a Mockingbird* invent false worlds, and their racism has been widely admired. Faulkner's and Lee's novels won the Pulitzer Prize, and these three novels together were on the *New York Times Book Review* bestseller list a grand total of 145 weeks. Just behind these books in widespread popularity are Jesse Hill Ford's *The Liberation of Lord Byron Jones* (a Book-of-the-Month Club selection), Shirley Ann Grau's *The Keepers of the House* (which also was awarded the Pulitzer Prize), Ben Haas's *Look Away, Look Away* (a Literary Guild selection), and Elizabeth Spencer's *The Voice at the Back Door.*[9] In novels in which race is not primarily the subject, the Negro is still portrayed somewhat more favorably than the white.[10] In Styron's *Set This House on Fire,* for example, a Negro family loves despite poverty and dirt, and the two whites involved in the racial episode hate. Brainard Cheney's *This Is Adam* creates a good Negro family and a good white aristocratic family; they oppose a world of conniving, dishonest white Snopeses. Mary Fassett Hunt's *Joanna Lord* and David McCarthy's mystery, *Killing at the Big Tree,* depict extremely good and extremely violent

Negroes. Yet passionate violence is about their only flaw. The significant evils in the lives of the Negroes in Lucy Daniels' *Caleb, My Son* and Paxton Davis' *The Seasons of Heroes* spring from the Negroes' relationships with the whites. In John Ehle's *Move Over, Mountain* Negroes tend to fall into two groups: the good, and those corrupted in the ways of Northern gangsters. In Marion Montgomery's *The Wandering of Desire* and William Hoffman's *A Place for My Head* white and black are both so evil that little good can be found to praise in either race. In only two Southern novels that I know is the white man on the whole almost as loving, as moral, and as good as the Negro—LeGette Blythe's *Call Down the Storm* and Hoke Norris's *All the Kingdoms of Earth*. Yet in neither of these does the fair treatment of each race result in really good fiction.

The most admirable trait of the Negro in all these novels is his ability and his willingness to love his fellow man. Over and over again love is treated as an issue of race. The Negro loves; the white hates. In William McIlwain's *The Glass Rooster* a white liberal leaves his Northern wife in the North and temporarily comes home. Among his white friends he finds little but hostility and hatred. Then he sees his old black friend Uncle Boo, who sweetly holds the "small body" of his grandson "pressed against his chest" (p. 56). The love of the Negro extends beyond the family to the white, and Uncle Boo welcomes Howard home with more genuine enthusiasm than any white friend has. Howard sees "the grin, wide as his hand, explode on the Negro's face, then burst in miniature on the lips of the child—as if that small face were an extension of Uncle Boo's" (p. 57). Tommy, Uncle Boo's son, has also just returned from the North. The father of the white hero, Howard, feels antagonized by his son, a liberal on the race question; Boo and Tommy adore each other.

Mary Fassett Hunt's *Joanna Lord*, though rather conserv-

ative, also sometimes portrays love as racial. Christmas in
the home of a white segregationist newspaper editor is unhappy. In the backyard cabin of the editor's black maid, she
is happy with her son and her lover even though they all
fear her violent husband. The decorations of the Christmas
tree in the white home are "synthetic" (p. 110). The tree in
the black home is "trimmed with a string of lights and fes-
toons of popcorn and tinsel. In the glow from the hearth it
enjoyed an added magic in the little room that Rachel kept
always neat and clean" (p. 111). Rachel's lover looks at her
with "an inexpressibly soft look," which she absorbs "as
though she had been caressed." Meanwhile back in the segregationist home several conflicts rage while the white
heroine of the novel remembers the look of love which she
had seen pass between the black maid and the yardman.

Perhaps the strangest case of love within a Negro family
in recent fiction is that in Lucy Daniels' *Caleb, My Son,*
which portrays filicide as an act of love. Asa, the murdering
father, demands respect, love, and authority in the family.
Caleb endangers the family by becoming a militant leader
and courting a poor white girl. In a ritualistic scene which
seems more African or Asiatic than American, Asa kills his
son. (Orientals have often held symbolic funerals for children who turned Christian, or even killed them.) To his
family Asa explains how he killed as an act of love: "Jake
White had shot his son," Asa said. "It was his right, son. . . .
It was his duty. You gotta give people plenty o' chance. . . .
But when they don' pay any heed, when they go right on
hurtin' people, it's yo' duty" (p. 116).

In this world where black is beautiful, the Negro family
in its beauty and goodness thrives on adversity, and racist
claims are made about the outstanding quality of love in
the Negro family. A white prostitute passes through a
Negro section of town and wishes "for the feeling of being
a part of something that you got from sitting around a table

in a family group like the people in these houses were doing" (*Watching at the Window*, p. 24). The black protagonist of *The Voice at the Back Door* fathered a child by an English girl in World War I and brought the child home with him. English girls, he says, do not love children as much as Negroes do. One of the most loving portraits of the Negro male is that of "our father" in Feibleman's *A Place Without Twilight*. He works for an angry restaurant owner who throws two books at him after "a waiter tripped over one and spilled a plate of soup" (p. 24). At home, "our father" drinks to dull his sensibilities so that he can tolerate his angry and puritanical wife. He loves his children and the books *John Keats, Poetical Works* and *Alice in Wonderland*. The Negro who seems the worst may often be truly good. Jewel, also in *A Place Without Twilight*, begs money and tells her friends, "Just to keep respectable," that it is for whiskey. Actually, she saves the money for doctor bills for her aged and syphilitic grandmother (p. 348). In the same novel Adelaide seems abominably selfish, but she endures almost unbearable suffering while her mother dies of cancer. She has no money to buy morphine to ease her mother's pain; so she gives herself to a lecherous doctor so that he will give her the prescriptions. Adelaide is a remarkable woman who happens incidentally to be a Negro (p. 301).

Sometimes the benevolence of the Negro characters resembles the sentimental and excessively romantic local color written by such nineteenth-century writers as Mary Noailles Murfree and Bret Harte. In Hoke Norris's *All the Kingdoms of Earth*, for example, a wife of a Negro soldier receives a telegram notifying her of her husband's death. She lives with her mother-in-law, who acts as if she is happy to hear of the death of her son. In disappointment and frustration the wife packs her clothes to leave and goes to tell the mother goodbye. She finds her leaning "against the wall, with her forehead against her arm. Her big, fat body was shaking, and her sobs were raw and ragged, like nothing Laura'd ever heard before." The wife "asked herself, How many times she hid herself like this and cried? How many times, Lord" (p. 202). Then the wife understands and returns to the house and unpacks. This is a superb scene, but in a way perhaps it is racist: it depicts a greater love between black and black than is ever shown between white and white in these novels.

The magnanimity of the Negro's love goes far beyond his own race. One Negro widower knits gloves for his white male friend.[11] When a liberal editor is stomped to death by whites, the Negro has "genuine grief" for him, a greater love for him than any white except his own wife. She says that a Negro says "the first thing anybody had said about Burke that made any sense."[12] Lucius, a white man in *A Dream of Mansions,* is grieved for by only one man, Adam Lincoln, the best Negro in the book (p. 159). Here the white denies grief, and the black is magnanimous with his. A loyal and old-fashioned Negro would kill a fellow black for his white employer. When Tom, the hero of *The Numbers of Our Days,* puts his children to bed, he leaves his wife in the living room alone with a Negro who has a Ph.D. degree. A Negro houseservant hides and watches with a gun to see that the well-educated teacher does not assault the wife (pp. 169–170). Apparently the white novelist in this ridiculous situation intends to emphasize the goodness and love of both Negroes.

Sometimes the white finds love in a relationship with a Negro when whites seem unable to love. The troubled wife of an unfaithful husband in *The Voice at the Back Door* visits an old Negro woman, Mattie, and feels immediate sympathy. Almost as soon as she saw her, "tears came easily, rushing, and fell warm on Mattie's hands and her own" (p. 169). And when husband and wife almost separate and leave small children untended, the Negro boy Bimbo tells stories to the white children. Patsy "was seated on Bimbo's knee, and was staring into his face like a devotee before an idol, and indeed she was to worship him, all her childhood long" (p. 169). No white man in these novels has love and sympathy as great as the good blacks have. Most white men hate Negroes. But Negroes love even dogs and enemies. A blind man in *The Liberation of Lord Byron Jones* has a selfless love for his dog. After a white man kills it while murdering a Negro, the owner of the dog buries it and says, "I'm making a little hump here. If I get lonesome I can come out and find where he is" (p. 310). The Negro hero, Huse, in *Look Away, Look Away* expects policemen "to kill him and yet he did not hate them" (p. 353).

> "Now you can beg if you want to," a cop said harshly from behind him. "Go ahead, coon, you got any begging to do, now's the time."
> Huse forced himself to stand erect. "I have no begging to do," he said. "But if you'll give me time, I'll pray for you."
> "Shit," somebody said from behind him. (p. 354)

The Negro is Christ-like, and the white Satanic.

Love and marriage or sterility may symbolize the goodness or the hardships of the Negro. Tradition, I believe, usually depicts sexual and love relationships between blacks and whites as casual and passing affairs between brutal white men and lustful Negro women. Not so the novels. The Negro woman is never casual. The white man rapes her, or she gives herself to him in pure love. Many of the Negroes in this fiction reflect the frustration and adversity of the race by being bachelors, old maids, widows, or widowers. Almost all the marriages between Negroes in the fiction are made in heaven. In *Look Away, Look Away* the traditional racial situation is almost completely reversed.

A gentle Negro leader of his people rejects a lustful mulatto
movie star, who is white in flesh and black at heart. Much
as he desires her, he rejects her because of the purity of his
love for his wife (pp. 447–448). Sometimes the "sense of
innate decency" of the Negro is saintly pure: Dandelion in
Byron Herbert Reece's *The Hawk and the Sun* turns his
eyes "from a wind-lifted skirt" (p. 22). The marriage between the white Will Howland and the Negro Margaret in
The Keepers of the House is the most perfect perhaps in any
modern fiction. They never have a single fuss. The relationship is so ideal that a grandchild thinks their "whole
room looked like a set, or a picture" (p. 177). Greater self-
lessness does not exist than that of the Negro mistress in
Robert Penn Warren's *Flood* who gave up her white lover
"because she didn't want" him to worry about "what some
Ku-Klux cretin might do to her" (p. 426). A liberal re-
porter in *Tiger in the Honeysuckle* has an affair with the
militant Negress Jonee, who is perfect in beauty, sex, and
love. The Negro mistress of a liberal banker in *All the
Kingdoms of Earth* is the most loving person in the book,
and her white lover is so frustrated over the impossibility
of living happily with her that he commits suicide. In *The
Voice at the Back Door* fidelity in the Negro mistress of a
white sheriff prevails over all: after the sheriff dies, a deputy says that his mistress will never take another man.

The goodness of a Negro woman's love for a poor white
is so exaggerated that the relationship is ludicrous in *The
Numbers of Our Days*. T. Joseph Clutts has a Negro mistress in his home, but he seals her off so that the world can
never even see her. Imprisoned, she still loves him. A racial
bigot and segregationist, he loves her. "Occasionally he
would even permit her to put her thick, Negroid lips to his
cheek, but he didn't encourage too much of that: there was
no need of letting her forget that she was a goddam nigger
and he was a white." Still she loves him! She is educated,

but he makes her "talk like a nigger mammy. . . ." And still
she loves him! In one of his moments of discouragement, he
says, "You're the only person in the whole damn world that
loves me. It's a goddam pity you're a nigger" (pp. 124–125).
Greater love has no woman than this, that she should give
up all self-respect for her lover.

Saintly and handicapped characters who are the victims
of white violence abound. Militant Negroes who fall at the
hands of whites in fiction are nonviolent and admirable.
Many of the victims who suffer most are innocent of any
kind of wrong. The real civil rights struggle in *Look Away,
Look Away* begins when a saintly Negro woman is arrested
for sitting in the wrong seat on a bus. She sat down far
enough toward the back when she boarded the bus, but
when more whites came she was exhausted and asleep and
did not hear the driver's first warning to move back. In one
riot whites deliberately shoot an old woman, as she says, in
the "privates," and she was merely attempting to put out a
fire.[13] The victim of lynching in *The Hawk and the Sun* is
crippled as well as mentally retarded.[14] The Negro boy
Sherman in *Clock Without Hands* is lynched because he is
guilty only of living in a house in a white neighborhood.
Both the white murderer and his Negro victim are carica-
tures. The Negro is as loving and cultured and intelligent
as the white is cruel and ignorant and stupid.

The kindly Lord Byron Jones is beaten to death by two
policemen because they are afraid that in his divorce trial
he will testify that one of the policemen is having an affair
with Jones's wife. Jones is kindly, lovable, intelligent, educated, courageous—all in all the most admirable person in
the novel. He offers to forgive his beautiful wife and take
her back even though she has told him, as she says, "forty
thousand God-damn times already" that she cannot give up
the policeman (p. 86). Married to such a woman and seeking a divorce, he still gently and virtuously remembers his

marriage and refuses the proffered love of a kindly prostitute.

Except for a useless arm, Tom Robinson in *To Kill a Mockingbird* is a handsome victim of the white man. He "was a black-velvet Negro, not shiny, but soft black velvet. The whites of his eyes shone in his face, and when he spoke we saw flashes of his teeth. If he had been whole, he would have been a fine specimen of a man" (p. 204). Tom escapes lynching and is sentenced to prison. Miss Lee has made the case so obviously unjust that even a Southern court in a novel could not execute him. Before his case is reviewed, Tom tries to escape and is killed. The only way for the novelist to untangle the plot was to let the victim kill himself off. The good and handsome victim is a device of racist propaganda: the more perfect the Negro, the more dreadful the white rapist, lyncher, or murderer.

The physical beauty of the Negro at least equals the beauty of the Southern belle in the romances about antebellum plantations. Negro women, one character specifically says, are more beautiful than white women: "their color made them more, not the less, women."[15] Even a Negro prostitute is idealized. A small woman, she has "a delicate, impassive face" and "fragile features."[16] Caleb is so handsome that "Women who did not know him could not keep their eyes from trailing him down a street" and so masculine that "men who did know him never quarreled with Caleb Blake."[17] Obviously, it would be easy to collect a few descriptions of whites with comparable beauty in thirty or forty novels *not* on the race question. But the beauty here is racist. These novels have few beautiful or handsome whites, very few. Beautiful or handsome Negroes are legion.[18]

One of the most blatant examples of slanting in favor of the Negro occurs in *To Kill a Mockingbird*. Two children who attend a Negro church are welcomed by the "warm bittersweet smell of clean Negro" (p. 128). But when a mob comes to lynch Tom Robinson, the same children smell "stale whiskey and pigpen" (p. 163). Fiction here is as absurd as some of the advertisements for deodorants. Smells have never been more political.

The black racism of Southern white novelists is painfully obvious in the way houses are described. Negro houses may be shabby or unpainted, but the Negro's love for his home is emphasized whenever a Negro house or section appears in a novel. Negro homes are painted, or the novelist indicates how the house is sound but unpainted. Flowers and well mowed or swept lawns beautify the houses. Churches and private schools are modest but neat and kept in good repair. Two homes smell of Negroes, perhaps because the Negro smell is foreign to the white. One Negro home smells bad after the Negroes move; another stinks perhaps symbolically because the woman who lives there is more loyal to whites than Negroes. Sometimes a novelist strains so hard that he tries to turn the ugly into beauty. In one Negro home "a single yellow bulb, dangling from a cord, sent a mellow glow over the scarred floor and pine walls."[19] A glare rather than a "mellow glow" comes from one naked bulb. Negroes who complain of selfish landlords would be surprised at how the white novelists have tried to compliment the race by surrounding their homes with beauty. Seldom does any novel treat slum filth. The circumstances of Negro life would certainly justify the subject, and the responsibility could be that of white landlords. But dirt and disorder would not be congruent with idealized Negroes.

In *To Kill a Mockingbird* the homes are simply unbelievable. Harper Lee does not find her native Alabama beautiful. Maycomb, she writes, "was spared the grubbiness that distinguished most Alabama towns its size" (p. 141). It does have one ugly house, however, and it belongs

to the poor white who falsely accuses a good Negro of rap-
ing his daughter Mayella. There are no screens, and the
yard is filled with gleanings from the city dump (p. 181).
Ewell lives close to the Negro section, where the "cabins
looked neat and snug with pale blue smoke rising from the
chimneys and doorways glowing amber from the fires inside. There were delicious smells about: chicken, bacon
frying crisp as the twilight air. Jim and I detected squirrel
cooking, but it took an old countryman like Atticus to
identify possum and rabbit, aromas that vanished when
we rode back past the Ewell residence" (p. 182). Strange
how even the cooking odors seem to turn up their noses
when they near a poor white.

The dress of the Negro follows the same pattern. Clothes
are ragged and drab only because of poverty, and seldom
then. Goodness and love of beauty are apparent in order
and cleanliness and colorful clothes. Negro children going
to bed at night leave their clothes "on a chair in a neat
pile."[20] That the novelist uses dress for racial propaganda
is apparent in abrupt juxtapositions of well-dressed Negroes and poorly dressed whites.[21] In *Joanna Lord* some
small Negro girls play on the sidewalk wearing colorful
pink and red dresses. Just before they appear, Mrs. Hunt
describes the poor taste of a wife of a candidate for governor: "she had no clothes that were right" (p. 69). And after
the passage about the little girls, the novelist calls attention
to a white woman who wears a drab dress. She says, "I have
no knack for clothes" (pp. 71–72).

The Negro in this fiction is thus superior to the white in
love, beauty, and love of beauty. He is also superior in en-
durance, manners, courage, religion, and even education
and intelligence. A young black man in *Memphis Jackson's
Son* thinks of a way to put out a forest fire. An aristocratic
white appreciates his advice, but a poor white is stupidly
angered: " 'Magine a nigger speakin up and tellin white

folks what to do" (pp. 191–192). When the protagonist of
A Place for My Head tries to browbeat his servant, he fails.
"Solomon usually beat him," the novelist says. "Like all
darkies he was quick to sense a weakness in a white man"
(p. 45). Overcoming all the handicaps a Negro has in deal-
ing with white businessmen, the black hero of *This Is
Adam* outwits a town full of scheming and dishonest whites
and saves his farm and that of an aristocratic widow. Ned
is the shrewdest character in *The Reivers*. Sherman, a blue-
eyed Negro in *Clock Without Hands*, has almost super-
human and clairvoyant intelligence. A pharmacist dying
of leukemia "stared into those blazing eyes and again he
felt that look of eerie understanding and sensed that those
eyes knew that he was soon to die" (p. 25).

These novelists never make a point of the superiority of
the white man's education over the Negro's unless it is to
the disadvantage of the white, who has, of course, the
greater opportunity. But several novels stress the superiority of a Negro character in education. The pastor of a Negro
church in the town of Gray's Landing in *The Numbers of
Our Days* has a Ph.D. in theology.[22] Elizabeth Spencer says
that the butler Robinson Dozer was "superior to all the
whites, for the Standsbury household was a sociable one—
not much given to books" (p. 246). The two most educated
native citizens of the town in Warren's *Flood* are a liberal
white lawyer and a Negro minister.

Part of the difficulty of the white novelist creating a
Negro character is obvious. Of course no white man can
get inside a Negro skin. More significant, he cannot even
get into the Negro's situation. The white novelist may con-
front a policeman, even be arrested. But he cannot be a
Negro who is arrested by a white policeman. The imagination of a novelist trying to portray a Negro confronting a
white policeman may exaggerate and falsify. Irene C. Edmonds, a Negro critic, thinks that even Faulkner created

stereotyped Negroes like Dilsey or symbolic ones like Sam
Fathers because he did not write from within the mind of
the Negro and so could not depict his thinking.[23] Few novelists have tried to write from such a point of view. Even
when Julia Peterkin and DuBose Heyward tried "to look at
life through the colored people's eyes and truthfully show"
what the Negro saw, the result could still be "just like any
white picture with a dark tinge."[24] Of course many good
novelists can write about racial subjects by using their
imagination. But when the white novelist in recent times
creates a Negro character, he also usually creates a racist
subject, and his Negroes think about racial things. The
most successful portrait of the Negro from the point of
view of the Negro in these novels is, I think, that of Cille,
a Negro girl in Feibleman's *A Place Without Twilight*.[25]
Unfortunately, in encounters between white and black
Feibleman nearly always oversimplifies and depicts an evil
white and a good black. Except when race is the subject
matter of the novel, however, no one could tell whether
Cille is Negro or white. And that is as it should be. The
heart is not black or white, but human. Cille is good not
because she is a Noble Savage, a Negro, but because of the
person she is. Feibleman's success in showing her as a person is his accomplishment. Sensitively, Cille loves and endures, admires the goodness of the parent she calls "our
father," and despises the puritanism of her mother. At the
end of the novel after her parents die, she washes the floors
and walls and furniture of her family home, stays in New
Orleans, and accepts her heritage. At one point in the
novel an ambulance comes to take her insane brother to an
asylum. Feibleman's account of Cille's feelings as the ambulance goes away is an extremely moving and sensuous
representation of the feelings of an emotionally stricken
woman without regard for race or color:

There was upwards of a hundred colored people, all ages, bunched close on Mama's dirt lawn and ragged sidewalk, spilling way out in the street. They muttered and whispered low to each other, and some to theirselves. Most of them kept their backs to me, watching the dust sucked up and swirled and left by the ambulance; but a few had already turned to look at the house.

I waited where I was.

I let the soles of my shoes knit into the floor of the gallery, and I waited right there where I was. I pushed down. I pushed all my juices down—down through my body, through my legs—around the bones through my ankles to my feet. Spurt by spurt, I pushed my juices out into the splintered, gray gallery floor. And I waited where I was.

I made us one, the gallery and me. For a few chiseled minutes, while my brother drove away with his secret and erased the air behind him—for those few minutes, I lent my own juices to Mama's gallery, and softened its floor with my life; I took its gray for my own. I changed that gray to steel. (p. 343)

Cille is a remarkably created woman. Feibleman can depict a heart, but the social relationships between white and black in the novel are false to the facts of Southern life and false as well to the human heart. The novel could be truly great only if race were not a primary issue. But it is. Almost all the things that Feibleman succeeds well with in the novel could be said about poor whites just as easily as about poor Negroes.

When a Negro is guilty of a wrong in a recent novel, usually the error can be blamed either on the white race or on the disadvantages which racism imposes on the Negro. The stereotype of what the Negro critic Sterling A. Brown has called the brute Negro has disappeared from fiction only to be replaced by the brute white. The evils of the Negro are usually of a certain kind—violence because of a racial situation and crimes of passion are probably the

most common. Often a wrong is not really a wrong, the
novelists suggest, because the white victim completely de-
served what he got.

Several novels depict a number of bad white people but
no bad Negroes and no wrongs committed by Negroes at
all: Byron Herbert Reece's *The Hawk and the Sun*, Lettie
Hamlett Rogers' *Birthright*, Walker Percy's *The Last Gentleman*, Norris Lloyd's *A Dream of Mansions*, and William Faulkner's *The Reivers*. In some of the novels errors
on the part of Negroes are inhumanly minor and incredi-
bly trivial. Whites attempt a lynching and wreak injustice
leading to death in *To Kill a Mockingbird*; but the only
error by any Negro occurs when Lulu objects to white
children attending her church: "You ain't got no business
bringin' white children here—they got their church, we got
our'n" (p. 129). And even this makes the Negro race look
better when all the other Negroes condemn her bad manners. Except for Beckwith Dozer, who turns out to be a very
good Negro at last, only one bad Negro appears in *The
Voice at the Back Door*, and her only trouble is that she is
"of a complaining nature" (p. 95). Peter S. Feibleman
creates whites who do evil things because they are white;
the Negroes in his novel are personally guilty of wrongdoing, but their errors are not attributed to their race.
Saintliness in the Negro is offset by one trivial error on the
part of only one Negro in several novels. One illegitimate
pregnancy is the only flaw in the Negroes of Reynolds
Price's *A Long and Happy Life*. Negroes in William Hoffman's *The Trumpet Unblown* are guilty merely of defending themselves from violent whites. Insanity causes all
the wrongs done by Negroes in *Watching at the Window*.
One remark costs a Negro leader the friendship of the good
white liberal in *The Numbers of Our Days*: he "made the
mistake of being a Negro first and a friend second" (p. 305).

There are few Negro mobs in fiction, and those which

do form are justified because of severe and immediate wrongs at the hands of whites. A Negro mob in *The Southerner* defends an innocent Negro from an angry white mob (p. 133) when the mayor and the governor refuse to send help. After long suffering and anguish caused by a town full of cruel and unjust whites, some Negroes riot violently in *Tiger in the Honeysuckle*, but otherwise this is a novel of perfect and idealized blacks.

In many novels wrongs suffered at the hands of white men cause Negroes to be unkind, bad-mannered, evil, and violently criminal. Negroes guilty of wrongdoing are still usually tender, kind, and loving. The crimes caused by something other than racial oppression are committed in anger. Some Negroes are hot-headed and passionate, but seldom is any Negro unkind or evil in cold, calculated premeditation. Thus even the Negro's crime can become symbolic of the white man's evil rather than of the Negro's. Sherman in *Clock Without Hands* acts not in anger but out of a deep-seated need to escape isolation and inadequacy. He hangs his employer's friendly dog. "Why don't nobody care about me? I do things, don't nobody notice. Good or mean, nobody notices. People pet that goddamned dog more than they notice me. And it's just a dog" (p. 216). Sherman's pitiful state is caused by the neglect of white men. He is lonely also because Southern white society unjustly executed his father for murder, and Sherman's own employer passed the sentence. The white's failure to recognize the Negro accounts for extravagance as well as violence. "Justify his two-thousand-dollar funeral," Jesse Hill Ford explains, "because until he died or was killed he was never once the center of attention before. Not once in his whole life" (p. 89).

White atrocities in *The Liberation of Lord Byron Jones* cause the reader to hope that the Negroes will wreak a terrible vengeance on the whites who wronged them. Henry Parsons beats his baby to death, even though he loves the baby, because of his wrongs at the hands of whites. Police had arrested him falsely when he inquired about a friend who was in jail, fined him, and extorted money from him, raped his wife, forced her at regular intervals to submit sexually to one policeman while another watched, and forced the husband and the wife to pay money to the police weekly. White persecution has so completely ruined Henry Parsons that even murder seems excusable; his wife says "he had to hit the baby boy" (p. 286). But he would have been a good man if it were not for evil whites. The gullible reader trapped into suspending his disbelief in this outrageous melodrama cheers for the Negro murderer Mosby when he throws the voyeur policeman into a hay baler: "He made two bales, part of him in one and part in another. He made two and a little bit more that the machine didn't know what to do with . . ." (p. 347). This is the poetic justice which the novel arrives at.

White novelists and their Negro characters find strange ways to blame whites for black excesses and crimes. The racketeer brother of the upright protagonist in Haas's *Look Away, Look Away* describes his profession and his way of living with the white man: "You got to come at them . . . from their meanness and greediness. There's two things that when people want 'em bad enough ain't got no color. One of 'em's a woman's twat and the other's money" (p. 46). The wild Saturday nights of drinking, "rape, assault, or murder" are also caused by racial oppression of black men. They seek "relief now from the tensions of grinding labor, of dirty or dangerous jobs in places no white man would go; relief from too much family and too little money and hope that went no further than to next payday" (p. 97). Jesse Hill Ford agrees. The white allows "the nigger" one Saturday night for "six days of his labor" (p. 89).

Black villains in this fiction are usually minor characters

only mentioned in passing. The novelist may hope that artistically a minor evil character will balance the sentimental portraits of good Negroes. The brother of the good Negro protagonist in Kiker's *The Southerner* is killed because he bragged about having loved another man's woman. He bleeds to death on the street after he is cut "to ribbons . . . in a herringbone pattern." "The cut on his throat was like two red parted lips" (pp. 17–18). In this novel Kiker is rabidly anti-white and pro-Negro, and somehow this Negro violence seems incongruent with his racial views. *Killing at the Big Tree* is a little less extreme. The small Negro boy Eli, who is thought to have witnessed the killing, is threatened by white and Negro. Conservative whites wish to kill a possible witness and to prevent a semblance of integration when the sheriff lets Eli stay at his house for a few days. This detective novel seems naively anti-Negro in the description of Eli's sister's boy friend, who kicks him, curses him, and threatens to cut his throat. "The alternative fighting and love-making over his head" goes on all through the night. A preacher who knows the family says that sternness has caused the violence in Eli's family. His older brother "was killed in a fight many years ago" (pp. 11, 13, 47, 126).

In *Joanna Lord* a jealous husband kills his wife and her lover. The novelist portrays the victims as loving, says that the crime was committed by a crazy man (p. 346), and draws no racial conclusion. A segregationist newspaper editor associates violence and race: "Crime of passion," he says. "A dime a dozen with niggers. *You* know that" (p. 348). At the end of the novel the editor renounces his racism. Probably the novelist does not intend this crime of passion to be regarded as racial; certainly the crime is not made as much a generalization as is the wonderful love between the slain couple.

Debased Negroes help to defeat their own race because

white men have succeeded in poisoning them with white
ideas. Some mulattoes resemble their white kin, love their
own whiteness, and hate their own race. A father tells a
Negro that he is too dark to marry his daughter. She says,
"I don't want a nigger baby!" Renegade Negroes and
Uncle Toms are most corrupted by the white man. In *The
Southerner* a Negro deliberately perjures himself and testi-
fies against his own brother to avoid losing his job in the
state highway department. "Here, at last," Kiker writes,
"was the perfect caricature of the Southern Negro, just the
bit of comic relief the trial needed, a flapping, fawning,
dim-witted sleepy-eyed Negro boy . . ." (p. 179). Robert
Penn Warren's character Jingle Bells is the most elaborate-
ly developed Uncle Tom in any recent Southern fiction.
In his job at a service station this student who grew up in
the North and who attends Fisk University is required to
wear a costume. He affects artificial manners and speech
the way "a jellyfish devours an oyster: it smothers it with
softness" (p. 9). In whispers he insults his customers. Perhaps it is the required abjectness which has destroyed him.
He is awarded a fellowship to attend the University of
Rome. "In Rome he would be himself, and that was what
was happening to him and would happen to him forever,
and, oh, he was not sure that he could bear it" (p. 366).
Jingle Bells has no identity, but his flaws are partly his own
doing.

In portraying a weak Negro character several novelists
have difficulty being fair to the race which they wish to
defend, idealize, and depict as nearly perfect. Ford, for example, is guilty of generalizing and name-calling when he
insults the Negro militants in his own novel. "Like the
cowards they were," he writes, "they didn't picket in front
of the locally owned groceries, only the chain stores. If they
picketed any other kind the owner might come out with a
gun. Somebody would be killed" (p. 83). In this passage

a Southern white novelist is rabid and militant enough to wish to send Negro characters to their deaths.

One novel in this entire mass of fiction attempts to portray at length a bad Negro character. Strip away the white race and the black mores from the fiction, and Feibleman's Negroes in *A Place Without Twilight* would not be distinguishable from whites. And that is as it must be in good fiction. Every race is human, though even the novelist needs constantly to be reminded of that simple fact. The evils of the main Negro family in the book spring from the mother, who is rigid, puritanical, intolerant, and fundamentalist. She made "the outside world . . . a don't" (p. 37) and "committed the crime of never staying happy" (p. 230). She is pleased when her loving but drinking husband dies and pleased again when her son is killed in the war because there was "one less person to have to be scared for" (p. 245). The sensitive daughter Cille, who hates her mother, still recognizes her mother's good intentions even when one of her brothers goes crazy. "And Mama meant right," Cille says. "The terrible part is, Mama meant right" (p. 122). The love of "our father," as Cille calls him, is as great as the frigidity of the mother. After a heart attack, he dies in a moment of defiance and even humor. "All right, now," he says to Cille. "Tell your Mama to get her ass out here. I'm on my way" (p. 48). More than any white novelist writing since 1954, Feibleman can see the Negro as a person instead of as a noble savage or a bad nigger.

Out of understandable sympathy, white novelists tend to provide the black man with excuses and justifications for all of his wrongs and his crimes. A downtrodden race, this fiction seems to argue, can do no wrong. Good fiction cannot be based on such moral disorder and oversimplification. Certainly there are excuses for many Negro crimes, but only a ridiculous fiction would attempt to forgive all of the blacks all of their crimes all of the time.

THREE

The White

PERHAPS NO OTHER PEOPLE HAS BEEN MORE THOROUGHLY detested by its own bards than Southern whites. It is as if the dramatists of Shakespeare's England had written one play after another about good Jews and bad Englishmen. In novels on the race question good whites are scarcer than good Germans and good Japanese in motion pictures about the heel-popping Nazis and the buck-toothed Japanese of World War II. One of Harper Lee's characters strongly objects to the persecution of Jews in Germany. "They're white, ain't they?" (p. 259). Persecution of Negroes, he implies, would be the thing to do.

Possibly guilt accounts for novelists' hatred of their own people. The fiction seems to argue that the white man is depraved because of the racial and political views of his heritage. Some novelists may get caught up in a wish to do something for the Negro. Moved by genuine feeling for human rights, they forget the requirements of good art. The propaganda may be almost unintentional with some. Others seem literally to nurture a deep hatred for Southern whites. Carson McCullers once told Ralph McGill that for years before she left the region she pointed her shoes north every night when she went to bed. She returned south occasionally, she said, to renew her "sense of horror."[1] Elizabeth Spencer libels her own state in *The Voice at the Back Door*. Yet she believes that her book is too optimistic: "even while I wrote it down," she has written, "the tenuous but

vivid thread of hope that I thought to be there had been
dissolving utterly."[2] Novelists may get trapped by their
own wish for approval, and condemning Southern whites
who are in conflict with blacks brings praise from a large
political audience. The Southern white can be attacked
with impunity.

The tragedy or the triumph of an underdog is always an
excellent subject for fiction, and the Negro is still cast in
that role. It is impossible to help him without opposing
the bully which has been keeping him down. Once a novelist is committed to praising the Negro as a noble savage, he
must also condemn the white. One oversimplification requires the other. Thus Ben Haas regards Southern history
as "A minority of sonsabitches so crazed on the nigger question that they're perfectly willing to take away everybody's
rights to settle it their way."[3]

Many writers strip off the mask of fiction and enter their
own novels to make generalizations which no reasonable
person could truly believe. Southern novelists now make
hostile statements which a few decades ago were attributed
only to silly and ignorant Yankees. "Lynching or football
game," according to Douglas Kiker, "it matters little—that
is September in the South."[4] No statistics, I suppose, could
convince this national newscaster and irresponsible novelist
that he is guilty of libel against millions of good people
who have not attended a lynching. In the six years before
the novel was published there were four lynchings in
America—one every eighteen months.[5] In one of these the
victim was a white man. If football were to correspond
with lynching, in some years there would not be a single
game in September or any other month. Mr. Kiker is given
to absurdities in fiction. He describes "a law of response"
to orators in the South. "You take any gathering of Southerners in any Deep South state—and they've got to be in a
gathering, mind you—and give them that same speech and

you'll get the same results every time" (p. 96). Kiker does not bother to differentiate between a meeting of Ku Klux Klansmen or a gathering of camellia growers or an audience listening to a lecture by Paul Tillich at Agnes Scott College.

In some novels everything—action, character, dialogue—centers on the question of race, and that in itself is a way for a novelist to make a generalization about the extremism of Southern minds. Characters think, talk, and preach about race. Consciously and unconsciously novelists often use a particular technique to make a trait regional. Several women in *Joanna Lord,* for example, talk about Joanna's husband's being unfaithful. "Joanna had felt the talk tonight . . . under the soft Southern voices of her friends, under their words and smiles and the warm pressure of their hands" (p. 9). The label "Southern voices" tends to make the hypocrisy and the cattiness of the women also Southern characteristics. In the same novel members of a post of the American Legion are called "boys," and the novelist casts a slur on their manhood in exactly the same way that a Negro man feels insulted when he is called "boy" (pp. 23–24).

Walker Percy flings mean generalizations. His protagonist, he writes in *The Last Gentleman,* "was the only white man in the entire South who did not know all there was to know about Negroes" (p. 194). Percy contends ironically here that no Southern white men know Negroes well and that all arrogantly believe they know everything. Percy is peculiarly vulnerable in his contention. He pretends to know the Southern mind—or what he might regard as the lack of one—as well as he says the Southerner pretends to know Negroes. Percy does not recognize his own arrogance. He continues: "A Southerner looks at a Negro twice: once when he is a child and sees his nurse for the first time; second, when he is dying and there is a Negro with him to

change his bedclothes. But he does not look at him during
the sixty years in between. And so he knows as little about
Negroes as he knows about Martians, less, because he knows
that he does not know about Martians" (p. 195). The
author does not confess what he does not know about
Southern whites.

Ralph Ellison has written that the Negro would not
recognize his humanity in modern American fiction. The
Southern white could not recognize his humanity, his society, or his history. "All that's left in the world," one of
William Hoffman's characters says, "is bastards."[6] And the
novel provides no contradiction to the statement. All
"country people" in a Southern state hate the Negro "to
the same degree" and, by implication, all once belonged to
the Ku Klux Klan.[7] Dullness and cruelty prevail in a town
in Arkansas so much that "A lot of people . . . needed that
secret thrill of miscegenation to whet the edge of their
lives. . . ."[8] Millions of Negroes have physical scars where
white men have cut them with knives.[9] And a good white
hero agrees that there are probably millions of white men
like the man who scratched a "cross about eight inches high
and six inches wide" on a Negro's chest. (The Negro's only
offense was that he had neglected "to take off his cap and
hold it in his hands" while his boss was passing by him.)
Some plantation owners did not physically punish slaves,
"but—they always made it a practice to hire overseers who
got a kick out of using the whip."[10] Thus, according to this
fictional history, Negroes were whipped on every single
Southern plantation that existed before the Civil War.

After two of William Styron's characters, Lonnie and
Cass, demolish a Negro home because the Negro cracked
a cheap radio without paying for it, Styron writes that
"they've got as many Lonnies and as many young Casses in
dear Old Dixie as they've got boll weevils" (p. 378). Lynch-
ers are ordinary Southerners;[11] even "reasonable people go

stark raving mad when anything involving a Negro comes up. . . ."[12] Novelists ridicule time-worn illogical generalizations about blacks. It is "accepted Southern opinion," for example, that "niggers are neither moral nor immoral. . . ."[13] Whites believe that every Negro man wants a white woman.[14] But novelists make the same kinds of sweeping fallacious statements about whites. The entire South is decadent; its "defeated spirit . . . invaded the souls of men like a secret, invidious disease."[15] Novelists who write statements like this are as narrow-minded as the racists they create in their fiction.

The main defenders of the established order in this evil and fictitious South are the politicians and the police. Most of them are cut to a similar pattern. It is easiest to see what they are in a full example, and possibly the worst is that in Jesse Hill Ford's *The Liberation of Lord Byron Jones.* Three policemen are characterized in the novel, and not one of them has a single redeeming trait. When a Negro is the victim of a crime, they ignore even beating, robbing, and misusing a woman (p. 26). One, Stanley Bumpas, beats a Negro nearly to death. All get confessions by using a cattle prod on a prisoner's testicles, fabricate evidence "often," and extort protection money. The Negro Mrs. Osborn paid the "sheriff in the place of Bumpas," and Bumpas "knocked the brains plumb out of" her (p. 66). For the rest of her life she looks like "something burnt in the fire" (p. 67). The worst policeman is Willie Joe Worth. He drove a school bus until he wrecked it while drunk on the job (p. 74); then he "got on as a helper on a beer truck, which was like turning mice loose in a corn crib . . ." (p. 76). After he lost that job, he became a policeman.

Willie Joe is sex crazy. He keeps his "left hand . . . between his legs. His right hand fondles his pistol" (p. 148). He stands naked before a mirror admiring himself as he wears his pistol on his hips. He was forced to marry his

wife; he slaps her; he does not want his little girls. His wife
wanted a son to name David, Willie Joe thinks, because
"probably she had been screwed one time by some traveling
salesman son of a bitch named David . . ." (p. 260). Willie
Joe plans to have his tubes cut so that he will have no more
children. His partner, Bumpas, is not quite as bad. He
"has two styles of driving, slow as possible and fast as possible" (p. 148). He has been eating baking soda for his
stomach and believes it has given him "cancer of the lungs"
(p. 263). He gets his sexual thrills from looking on while
Willie Joe has relations with Negro women.

When a Negro telephones about getting his brother out
of jail, Willie Joe and Bumpas arrange to meet him on the
corner of a street. Willie Joe hits him nine times with a
blackjack and arrests him for being drunk even though the
Negro is a teetotaler. When Henry's wife calls about getting him out of jail, the two policemen drive her out in the
country, threaten to arrest her, park between barrow pits
so that she cannot run away. Willie Joe forces her to give
herself to him so that her husband will not be kept in jail
interminably. Mr. Stanley Bumpas watches intently and
with "satisfaction." This episode, Willie Joe says, is only
"the down payment on the bill" (p. 156). Her husband will
get out of jail, but he will be arrested again any time his
wife refuses the demands of Willie Joe.

Back at the jail the policeman at the desk fines Henry
thirty-five dollars, gives him a false receipt for that sum,
writes a receipt for five dollars in the official book, lets
Henry pay five dollars a week for twelve weeks (sixty dollars in all), and plans to distribute the fifty-five dollars
graft between the three policemen. In frustration and tor-
ment sometime later the Negro kills his baby. "Maybe you
can't believe it," his wife says, "but Henry love this baby"
(p. 286).

Willie Joe is also carrying on an affair with the wife of

the Negro undertaker Lord Byron Jones, who is, as said before, more sensitive, cultured, and intelligent than any white man in the novel except for one liberal who has a Northern wife. When he visits her, he walks in the house without knocking, Ford says, "in the way any white man enters any nigger house" (p. 180). When the Negro husband comes home, Willie Joe tells him, "Well, you better watch, by God, the way you walk in a house without knocking. . . . I don't like nobody sneaking up on me" (p. 186). When Willie Joe learns that his Negro mistress is pregnant, he slaps her three times and then chops "a blow to her solar plexus—the finishing touch by the master mechanic" (p. 268). Her husband will sue for a divorce unless she agrees to give up her white policeman lover. After he refuses to drop the divorce case which would publicize Willie Joe's relationship to a Negro woman, Willie Joe and Bumpas stomp him to death. Bumpas castrates the corpse to make it look as if another Negro had killed him for having an affair with his wife. They come back to the policeman at the desk and explain their long absence: "We had to kill a nigger. . . . You can't accomplish nothing like that in five minutes you know" (p. 315).

Willie Joe turns himself in to the drunken mayor and the city attorney. The mayor wishes to prosecute some innocent person instead of the guilty policeman, but the attorney tells Willie Joe, "So maybe you have made a little mistake. At least now you've learned your lesson. More than one man has slipped off the straight and narrow when he wasn't thinking. . . . I'd say you've killed a man in the line of duty. Is that so bad for a police officer?" He advises the murderer to *"go on just like nothing happened"* (pp. 334–335). Some poetic justice is achieved when Willie Joe worries himself into suicide and Bumpas is killed by a wronged Negro who throws him into a hay baler.

These three men are the only police described in the

novel. Ford writes nothing good about any policeman. Neither human nature nor the facts justify such an incredible portrait. Ford's book so oversimplifies human nature that it has no credibility. Yet Granville Hicks regards this novel as "the most exciting and the most enlightening novel of our times about the race conflict in the South."[16] This appalling bigotry arrives at a dreadful regional and sociological generalization without making even a gesture toward considering the facts. In 1968 I had lunch with Robert Penn Warren, Eugene Patterson, and Ralph McGill. Mr. Patterson asked Mr. Warren whether he had read *The Liberation of Lord Byron Jones.* Mr. Warren had not. After I objected to its many distortions, Mr. Patterson expressed his belief that the novel is an accurate portrait of the South and of Southern policemen. It is hard to believe that even the author of this novel regards it as having a sound basis in reality. When a native small-town Southerner, the distinguished former editor of the *Atlanta Constitution* and the present editor of the *Washington Post*, believes the absurdities in this novel, one wonders how truth itself can ever prevail.

Police in Southern fiction are bad mainly because they are white. The savagery of policemen like Willie Joe is the novelist's way of justifying the Negro, who must endure without being able to defend himself. The more fanatic the novel, the worse the police. Two officers in *The Glass Rooster* are almost as violent as Willie Joe Worth. In *Clock Without Hands* a sheriff allows a lynch mob to use his hat in drawing lots to see who will bomb a Negro house. In *Look Away, Look Away* the white political power structure invites a colonel to come into the state and "start a war" with the Negroes (p. 488).

"I have never met a truthful cop," a white girl says in Lillian Smith's *Our Faces, Our Words*; "there may be some somewhere, I'm sure there are a few in Atlanta, or Richmond, maybe in North Carolina or Tennessee; but I have never come near one in the movement."[17] This is an inaccurate social generalization rather than a truthful philosophical statement about the honesty of men. Even if it were true that all Southern policemen are incurable liars, novelists could not hope to write about them and have credible human characters. Yet they have tried to do so. In fourteen Southern novels every action by every policeman carrying out his duties is dishonest, evil, brutal, or violent.

Bad as Willie Joe Worth is, he does not by any means exhaust all the ways in which policemen do wrong to Negroes in this fiction. Police do not try to catch murderers or dynamiters of Negroes. They bootleg whiskey and take money from bootleggers, act cowardly in violent situations, aid and abet lynching, regard Negroes as animals but not human beings, try to kill liberal reporters, laugh at stale jokes told by their superiors, give a driver's license to a Negro who drives poorly but tells sexy stories about Negro women, fail another Negro driver because he has his color on his shoulder, arrest a newspaper publisher because he has been hit on the head with a rock thrown by a segregationist, hunt innocent Negroes to shoot or execute them for crimes they did not commit, shoot a sharecropper because he leaves without paying his debt (this policeman was almost afraid to tell his father he had shot the man), refuse to protect white women and children from a mob which is burning a barn and killing animals, protect the mob from the woman, beat people and jail them for playing cards. And this list of the awful crimes of police does not take into account the repetitions of Willie Joe's crimes that occur over and over in these novels.

The evil policemen are thus stereotypes. Even their appearances reflect brutality or eccentricity or stupidity. The officers in *Tiger in the Honeysuckle* are so ridiculous that they could attract crowds in a circus. One constable wears

a "five-hundred-dollar toupee" (p. 128). A detective has a
crewcut and has "upside-down eyebrows," and another is
a "small blond." "Neither detective," the novelist says,
"could track an elephant in the snow" (p. 216). The county
juvenile officer cracks his neck. "That is to say, he actually
seized himself by the chin and the back of the head at intervals of thirteen minutes or less and proceeded to pop the
knuckles of his neck-bones, as if he were a chiropractor"
(p. 148). One writer and even the "naive natives" in his
novel can recognize "ex-cops" by "some definite something
in their faces."[18] The policeman tends to be "meaty," and
the "hog's eyes" set in "the red fat on his face" are "small
and cruel"; his mouth is cruel.[19] The sheriff who beats a
Negro girl with a billy stick in *Clock Without Hands* has
"dainty purplish hands and a broken nose" (p. 221). Physically the white Southern enforcer of the law is often freak-
ish in some way which symbolizes his depravity. One
redeeming feature of this abominable fiction is its un-
conscious humor.

When the police in a novel are not all bad, they tend to
fall into other patterns. A few novelists make mere ges-
tures toward some balance of morality. The numerous bad
law men in *Tiger in the Honeysuckle* are offset by one good
policeman, but he is killed. Policemen who derive from a
sharecropper heritage in Gwaltney's *The Yeller-Headed
Summer* resemble Willie Joe Worth, but one policeman
does do one good thing when he prevents a lynching. The
sheriff in *To Kill a Mockingbird* is one of the good guys,
but he is portrayed almost as a sidekick of the perfect and
sentimentally drawn Atticus. Policemen in *Watching at
the Window* are kind to an insane Negro. Faulkner in *The
Reivers* creates one stereotyped brutal Southern policeman
and one saintly constable. The stereotyped liberal and the
policeman are combined in one character in *Killing at the
Big Tree* and *The Voice at the Back Door*. In both he is

surrounded by other law men who resemble Willie Joe Worth. With few exceptions, Southern policemen in recent fiction are poisoned with race hatred, as brutal as the Gestapo, as sex crazy for black women as any goat or satyr, as immoral and unprincipled as a Hollywood oriental diplomat.

Madison Jones's *An Exile* and Robert Penn Warren's *Flood* reveal how officers of the law can be depicted without prejudice, hostility, or sentimentality. Jones's sheriff is painfully torn between loyalty to his office and the bribe of a girl's love to get him not to arrest a bootlegger. He is tormented by his conscience. Race is not an issue in the novel. In fact, the cast of characters is entirely white. But the point is that to be convincing a character, whether he be a policeman or a king, black or white, must be studied with some understanding of human nature. In contrast, few policemen in novels about race ever feel the slightest guilt or uncertainty. They are pasteboard figures without reality. Jones's sheriff decays morally and falls, but at the end of the novel in a tragic death he again deserves the honor of the title of his office, sheriff. Sylvester Purtle in *Flood* once tried unsuccessfully to prevent a mob from lynching a Negro. When he recovered from the beating he had received, he arrested "the one man he had identified." The man was acquitted, but Purtle was re-elected because of his "published statement" that he "would arrest any man without fear or favor or die trying." The ways of his electorate, Warren says, are "inscrutable" (p. 90). Another officer in *Flood* is the deputy warden of the state penitentiary. He has wisdom, but he says "nigger" instead of "Negro." In most recent Southern fiction he could not say that without being thoroughly corrupt. The deputy tells Pretty-Boy, a Negro waiting for execution, that he is going to make it, going to be a man, going to walk to his own execution. He has respect for the condemned Negro's manhood utterly without regard for his race or his crime. The recognition of the inscrutability of a fallen sheriff, a courageous officer of the law, an uneducated warden, and the electorate of a small Southern town makes for good fiction. Without that complexity man possesses no manhood. It is strange that in defending the Negro most white novelists do to the white policeman what they accuse the white policeman of doing to the Negro—they deny him manhood and human status.

Like all other evils in the world, unjustified violence in these novels is almost invariably caused by whites. In physical confrontations with Negroes, policemen lead the segregationists. Except for the good liberal, all other kinds of whites resemble the brutal police. Employers and bosses are unusually hard-hearted. Sam Deal in *Look Away, Look Away* forces a Negro to work in a dangerous ditch after a rain. A cave-in kills him, and when his fellow workmen dig him out, Sam says, *"calm as if he in church, Well, we done killed us a nigger."*[20] Appropriately, Sam later becomes police commissioner. Preachers and businessmen in fiction are also hostile to the Negro race. Except for a very few liberals, those ministers and businessmen who do not actively fight the Negro will not lift a hand to preserve his rights or even to save him from violence.[21]

Modern Southern novels on the race question are as violent as the wildest yarns of the frontier or the bloody stories about Indian captives in early America. Even when fiction is extravagant and incredible, it still grips the attention of the reader with a great suspense, even anxiety at times. A reader who is aware of the sentimentality of a novel can still vacillate between emotion and moments of near-humor when the writer goes to extremes. Likewise, in this sociological fiction the reader can be gripped for a time by the violence until he recognizes the absurdity of the author's abuse of the truths of the heart and of the facts.

Sometimes the tone becomes ridiculous. In Walker Percy's *The Last Gentleman* a policeman bursts into a house filled with Northern whites interested in civil rights. Immediately he asks, "Where's the poontang?" (p. 324). Then in a "routine voice" Beans Ross says, " 'All right, Breeze,' . . . not looking at him." Sweet Evening Breeze takes off his stocking cap. "Hardly watching but with a quick outward flick of his wrist, Beans hit Breeze on the forehead with the blackjack. Breeze fell down." Then the policeman again obscenely calls for women. This absurdity seems not to be a comic parody of anything. Percy apparently intends it to be a representation of everyday modern Southern society.

Among the many privileges of the whites in this group of extraordinary novels is crime. In thirty novels I counted 132 acts of violence and serious crimes by white men. I cannot remember a single white criminal who is punished by the law. These figures do not include the numerous instances of bootlegging and drunken driving. Nearly all the victims are upright liberal whites or noble blacks. White criminals sometimes wish to gain materially, but more often the motive is simply to hurt or kill Negroes. These are bloody books. I know of no other literature in which crime and violence are so gratuitous and so completely without reason. Of the 132 crimes, there are sixteen instances of murder,[22] and this counts the murder of twelve Negroes at one time as only one instance of crime. How many hundreds of people are killed it would be difficult to determine. White people are guilty of nineteen assaults and knifings, and again frequent assaults over a period of days on one victim by several attackers are counted as one crime. There are two murders by dynamite; eight instances of intent, threat, or attempt to murder; three lynchings; five attempts to lynch; six instances of manslaughter (one in which a drunken driver kills five Negroes and is not arrested because the sheriff is paid money by the bootlegger who sold the driver the whiskey); seven suicides (usually of good whites overwhelmed by a race problem); a threat to murder the president of the United States. Sex crimes include eight rapes, a sexual assault on a Negro boy by a white man, sodomy, castration, and a threat of castration. In riots and mobs, whites kill, dynamite, burn, run people out of town because of the race question, break up property. Firemen refuse to fight fires in the Negro section of a town. Whites extort, swindle, bribe, refuse to pay income tax. The white men's courts wrongfully imprison and carelessly err in executing Negroes.

It might seem that crime and violence are a proper province of the novelist, who may select moments of crisis in order to reveal the human heart in its deepest struggles. Does Southern fiction which is not on the race question contain just as much violence as is found in these thirty novels? No. Most of these novelists have written other novels which contain less violence. The proof of the prejudice of these novels is in the fiction itself. The Negro is not criminal and violent. In contrast with the whites in fiction and with the statistics about Negro crime in America, the lack of crimes committed by black men in these books is absurd. Only about thirty-two instances of crime by Negroes compare with 132 by whites. Ten of these are killings which the novelists present as understandable because of infuriating crimes previously committed by whites; three cases of violence result from insanity more than criminal tendency; two Negroes become involved in gambling and the numbers games but later succeed in overcoming their weaknesses; three violent crimes of passion result from the Negro's sexual jealousy, which seems excusable because of his ardency; three instances of mob violence occur because the Negro responded only after he had been persecuted by white mobs; whites hire a Negro to kill another

Negro; and in two instances so little information is given that it is impossible to tell the motive or reason for killing. In thirty novels about the race question there are numerous Negro characters but only about a half dozen violent crimes without provocation enough to make them seem understandable. These compare with 132 white crimes. These novels are written by authors ostensibly dedicated to the task of ending racism. Without proper regard for the truth or the facts, they leap into the fray. The irony is that statistics on the crimes committed by characters in their novels prove that they are seeking to end racism and prejudice by using tactics which are extremely prejudiced and racist.

Crimes represented by statistics have no life's blood or death's blood. After knowing how bad the white is and how good the black, the reader must turn back to the crimes themselves. Several novels intensify the evil of the white and the good of the Negro by making the blacks in certain families fall victim to crime in ways similar to the fates of their ancestors. A hideous crime against a Negro is described early in the novel, and then references to it appear over and over as a refrain which haunts the modern Negro leader who will probably share his ancestor's fate in the catastrophe at the end of the novel. The many allusions to this crime set an atmosphere or tone of suspense and horror for the reader. The victimized ancestor of the heroic leader Huse in *Look Away, Look Away*, for example, is his Uncle Mason Jar, who earned his nickname because he had to drink a pint Mason jar full of liquor so that his white boss would not lose a five-dollar bet. The Negro is a teetotaler. The white man bet that the Negro could drink a pint of whiskey and go on with his work. If the Negro does not try to drink it, the white man will cut him with a knife. The white has filled the jar with kerosene. The Negro drinks it and is sick for the next two weeks. Every time he feels sick on the job, his boss asks whether he needs another Mason jar.

Still the evil white man has not had all the sport he wishes. He demands Mason Jar's wife, and the Negro waits while his boss enjoys her. Thelma tells him that "It don't touch me, not the part of me loves you. Please. Don't you see, there ain't no way to help it?" (p. 78). After "many times," however, Mason Jar decides that his wife loves her rapist's "whiteness," and he burns them alive in a cabin. Three whites shoot him down. The one with a double-barreled shotgun is "squinting, grinning," and they drive away from Mason Jar's body with a "whoop, a shrill high cry."

Several Negro victims of crimes have ancestors who have suffered in ways similar to this. Beck Dozer's father in *The Voice at the Back Door* was killed when a group of whites killed twelve Negroes because they wished to establish a school; a child harassed by segregationists kills himself as his liberal father had before him in *Birthright*; Sherman in *Clock Without Hands* is lynched, and his father had been unjustly executed. The judge who sentenced his father later treated Sherman with excessive kindness and then made the speech which caused a mob to lynch him. The tragedy that runs in families emphasizes the psychology of a leader-victim, but more than that, it stresses the inhumanity of a white community which harasses the same Negro family generation after generation. Tragedy seems greater when the same catastrophe recurs in the same family, as when the coffins of two sons killed in a war arrive home at the same time. For the purposes of propaganda the novelists use this repeated pattern to prove the violence of the white and the benevolence of the suffering black.

Sex without love is lust or prostitution. Depicting sex in literature merely for the purpose of causing sexual excitement is pornography. I do not know the word which

names the way sex is abused in these novels. The stereotyped situation in legend has always been that of a pure
woman raped by a brute Negro who is then lynched. This
is often the false invention of a racist mind. That is not the
case in this fiction. Not one Negro man rapes a white woman. Yet, in 1965, 4665 Negro men in America were arrested
on a charge of forcible rape compared to 4485 whites.[23]
Negroes comprise about ten percent of the population but
apparently rape nearly as much as all other races combined.
Here the novelists have simply ignored the facts. In this
fiction bad white men force themselves upon good Negro
women. The only white women who have sexual relationships with Negro men love them. Bad whites falsely accuse
good and kindly black men of rape.[24] Whenever the subject
of race is involved in an extramarital sexual relationship,
there is true love if the white is a liberal and lust or rape
or hatred or wrong if the white is a segregationist. The
purest characters are the liberal men who resist sexual
temptation because of their devotion to pure and beautiful
wives. The happiest affairs are those between good white
men and black women (who are always good).[25] Sometimes
love for a Negro woman makes a man more broadminded;
the rabid segregationist T. Joseph Clutts in *The Numbers
of Our Days* is converted into a liberal by love. But Oman
Hedgepath in *The Liberation of Lord Byron Jones* gives
up his Negro lover and wonders how he ever loved her. In
numerous sexual relationships between Negro and white
in all this fiction no one Negro ever molests or harms a
white. Nor does any Negro ever love less than his white
partner in the affair. Whites lust, talk obscenely in public,
indulge in sexual perversion, beat, rape, and kill. Those
who are not criminally oversexed are sterile. One Southerner tries to kiss his girl Laura Lee, whom he has courted
for years. When she refuses he says, "We've got to do something."[26] But they can think of nothing to do. A novelist

carried away with himself writes how segregationists breathe obscenities "down the cleft" between the liberal heroine's breasts. That is an absurd image, especially since the woman is in a public store and does not wish to be breathed on.[27] In Lillian Smith's *One Hour* a white janitor is angered because Negro medical students see breast tumors which have been removed from white women. He blows up a house in retaliation.[28]

An extraordinary theory about a cause of homosexuality is suggested by those Southern novelists who conclude that it is the result of the white man's treatment of the Negro. A drunken Negro in *Look Away, Look Away* argues that "the Negro-withdrawn-from-society" disengages himself and "turns homosexual or something" (p. 438). An unhappy relationship with an extremely puritanical mother apparently is one cause of Clarence's homosexual relationships with white men in *A Place Without Twilight*. The Negro orphan victim in *Clock Without Hands* was assaulted when he was eleven. His white friend, grandson of a coarse and gross segregationist, can make love to a prostitute only because he has in mind the "dark face" of his Negro friend. An excessively masculine racist father attempts to convince his son that the boy has killed a deer; and the father tries to bathe him in the deer's blood. Aggression toward the good and the gentle often corresponds with aggression toward the Negro.

Whites wish first to beat or kill or castrate Negro men and second to make love to Negro women. Many novelists use sex to create a false and vicious society. Southern fiction on sex and race has gone mad. In *Look Homeward, Angel* Thomas Wolfe wrote of a white father's love for his unacknowledged Negro son; now it is more typical for the novelist to create a character like the white owner of a slave who rapes her and then kicks her off the lounge in his office. After the baby is born, he says, "Keep that little yellow bastard out'n my sight. . . . If'n you don't I'm goin' to feed 'im to the hawgs."[29]

Unprovoked hatred of Negroes, violence, crime, and sexual aberrations are only the most obvious characteristics of segregationist Southerners. All kinds of technical niceties are used to prove the inferiority of the white race. Absurd if not insane social manners and conventions prevail in white society in fiction. The critic cannot prove that they are untrue or that they never happened. All he can do is maintain that the convention is not a part of his experience of the South in his own life or vicariously. This fanatical sociology cannot be refuted because the rebuttal would have to encompass all knowledge and all episodes before the refuter could say a thing did not and does not happen.

Instead of seeing the humor, the depth, and the foibles of Southerners in the way the best writers have (Faulkner, Warren, Wolfe, Welty), these novelists are closer to the fiction of, say, Sinclair Lewis. Douglas Kiker, for example, creates a judge in a modern city the size of Atlanta, Birmingham, or Richmond. This jurist says *far* for *fair*, calls a grown Negro man "boy" in court, and spits "discreetly in the spittoon beside his chair. . ." (p. 161). (The adverb *discreetly* is hostile to the judge.) Kiker has made him pompous while he engages in an activity considered filthy in recent times. The restaurant "Grits 'n Gravy" charges "sky high prices" for "authentic Southern food" (p. 287). "It was a favorite of the ex-farm boys who had come to the city and got rich." So far Kiker has indicated that the country has not been taken out of the boys, that they are willing to be exploited and to pay high prices for inexpensive food. They eat food "they had been brought up on and had never quite managed to lose their taste for. . . ." By either Kiker's standards or the hypocritical standards of ex-farm Southerners, Southern food is wrong because these men have been trying to give it up. They seem to overdress in "expensive, tailored clothes" although their dress and their manicures are incongruous compared with "their big, red, workingmen's hands." This is a kind of snob appeal which may even result in some gullible Southern readers being unconsciously influenced to think that they should change their diet as well as their views on race. It simply shows that Kiker cannot be trusted in the novel to give a fair picture of Southern life.

Impolite language and obscenity are used for shock value and propaganda. A segregationist in *Look Away, Look Away* states one of the most common Southern attitudes toward the use of the word *nigger*: "Only white trash call them niggers where they can hear it" (p. 184). But the only Southerners who consistently avoid the term in this fiction are liberals. One novelist uses the term in application to a white man. Poor whites in William Hoffman's *A Place for My Head* speak "in the slow, almost niggerish fashion of the county . . ." (p. 33). No race could be pleased by the remark. The term *nigger* is associated with other insults when bad poor whites talk to good blacks. One white woman tells a Negro girl that she hears that a father disowns a Negro woman for being a virgin at sixteen; and when the Negro replies, the white says, "Don't you talk back to me, you nigger slut. . . ."[30] Whites have no regard for the feelings of Negroes. Customers in a beauty parlor where a Negro is a "girl Friday" "would not have bothered to soften their voices to say anything they had to say about her."[31] Whites, on the other hand, are ridiculous in the way they take offense when blacks do not intend to offend. A white man in *Move Over, Mountain* says that he cannot remember "much o' anything" (pp. 58–60). Trying to be agreeable, a Negro responds by saying, "I don't remember well, either." The *either* offends the white, who now starts contradicting himself and arguing that he has a good memory. No black man should cast a slur upon a white even when it is the truth admitted by the white.

Negroes and liberals never speak obscenely, but segregationist whites of all social classes speak in the foulest language in the presence of women, at parties, and in public meetings. One aristocratic mother of a segregationist leading citizen has an automobile accident which is her fault. The author calls attention to a regional flaw; she talks in an "outraged Southern voice" to a truck driver from Chicago: "You son of a bitch! Don't you know you're talking to a lady!" Being a Northern gentleman, the driver calmly asks: "What is this—America?" Here Jesse Hill Ford suggests that violent cursing prevails in the South as opposed to "the truck driver's thick arms, a raised gesture replacing words . . . , Chicago style" (p. 117).

The Southern politician is either a stereotyped demagogue or a liberal. Sometimes he reforms his political views toward the end of a novel. Judge Fox Clane in *Clock Without Hands* is one of the most contemptible political figures in all these novels. He has almost all the flaws that he possibly could have. This ex-congressman and present candidate for congress is "an enormous man with a red face and a rough halo of yellow-white hair. He wore a rumpled linen white suit, a lavender shirt, and a tie adorned with a pearl stickpin and stained with a coffee spot" (p. 12). Despite his weight of 310 pounds he says he is not fat, "just stout and corpulent" (p. 49). He journeys to Johns Hopkins for medical treatment but neglects to send his daughter-in-law, who dies of a rare disease. Inconsistently, he has his tooth pulled by "the best mule doctor in the county" (p. 50). He smells sweaty. He eats greedily, begins drinking early on Sunday morning. He curses the federal government, promises to introduce a bill to "redeem all Confederate monies, with the proper adjustment for the increase of cost-of-living nowadays" (p. 37), refuses to pay income tax or social security for his maid, says that justice "is a chimera, a delusion" (p. 40), although he has been a judge. He bans a book from the public library but puts a book cover for *The Decline and Fall of the Roman Empire* around the *Kinsey Report* to keep anyone from knowing that he is reading such salacious material. He regards mill-workers as "the emotional scum of the earth" but owns a great hunk of Wedwell Spinning Mill stock (p. 102). His flaws stress and emphasize the error of his violent segrega-tionist views. He insults a Negro from Cuba visiting the House of Representatives, sentences a good Negro to death for killing a bad white man in self-defense, wrongly sen-tences another Negro to death (pp. 180–181), makes a speech agitating for the lynching of his own favorite ser-vant for the crime of renting a house in a white district. The novel ends on the day when the Supreme Court gave its 1954 ruling about the public schools. The judge is asked to speak against the court on the radio. He recites the Gettysburg Address while an announcer punches him, try-ing to indicate that he is saying the wrong things. On the last page of the novel, the judge speaks, "It's just the other way around! I mean it just the other way around!" (p. 241). The South has its demagogues, but such extreme cases as this live only in the mind of a Southern white novelist.

The stupidity of the Southern political official is even evident in the state of public architecture. As expected, the horrors of public buildings reflect the extent of the novel-ist's outrage about attitudes toward race. *Tiger in the Honeysuckle* is one of the novels most bigoted against the South. City hall in that novel has "three decks of jaundiced brick and pigeon droppings, fluted white hollow columns of galvanized metal . . ." (p. 31). Cheap materials here are supposed to symbolize a pretentious aristocracy. In the same town water squirts through the ceiling of the court-house and into the courtroom so badly that it requires the janitor, the maid, and all the officers of the law to empty

"buckets and tubs."[32] Elizabeth Spencer cites a study showing that "only five jails in the state of Mississippi took an
unskilled person of average intelligence more than twenty
minutes to break into or out of" (p. 97).

Over and over again novelists use the pathetic fallacy of
a sterile, dry, hot, insufferable setting to reflect the sterility
and tempestuousness of a typical segregationist situation
and temperament. Even when a novelist describes the
Southern landscape as rich, fertile, and varied apart from
the race question, he still uses hostile geography when race
is his subject. Often a book begins with an unflattering
description of setting. The first sentence of *The Voice at
the Back Door* describes heat, drought, and dust "gushing."
Feibleman's *The Daughters of Necessity* begins in "a paved
dampish swampland place, set by a nameless bog along the
ragged lower part of the eastern United States."[33] The action of William Humphrey's *Home from the Hill* starts
with "a dusty long black hearse" sitting "under the shadow
of the Confederate monument."[34] Southern climate is the
object of the hatred of a dying character on the first page
of *Clock Without Hands*. Death will prevent him from
spending his retirement years in Maine and Vermont.
He is doomed to live out his few remaining days in a land
where he is "tired of sun and glare."[35] An incident of racial
violence in Styron's *Set This House on Fire* is introduced
with all the trappings of a stereotyped Southern world: a
"sweltering one-horse movie house," "summery-smelling
mimosas," "dust rising from the scorched back alleys of the
town, and old ladies fanning themselves on front porches
drenched in green shadow, and mockingbirds caroling
thunderously . . . purely summer, purely southern . . ."
(p. 371).

The first scene in *A Place for My Head* is set in the main
gathering place in town, a drugstore. "From the ceiling
three shaky, slow-moving fans stirred the hot summer air

to no coolness. The voices of the men at the imitation-
marble counter rose angrily. On the table before Angus
two flies moved sluggishly over spilled sugar" (p. 13). This
passage contains many social criticisms of citizens in this
Southern community. The inadequate fans indicate that
they have not had the energy and ingenuity to get a machine adequate to counteract the heat. The men do not
control their tempers. The store has cheap imitation
furnishings. No one keeps out or kills the flies. One fly
might with luck avoid a diligent swatter; two flies suggest
no swatter at all. If anyone wished, the flies could be easily
killed because they are sluggish. And perhaps their inertia
reflects the laziness of the people. No one cleans up the
spilled sugar. Despite all these atrocious surroundings, this
is the main gathering place of the community. It is logical
to presume, therefore, that the same kinds of problems exist in most of the homes in the town.

The South in these books is a great cultural wasteland.
When a radio plays "music unbroken"—without "jabber-
ing" and "yammering"—a character concludes that the
program comes from a "Midwestern or Northern station."[36] Walker Percy is especially satirical toward a modern Bible belt South. A traveler going South sees "more and
more cars which had Confederate plates and plastic Christs
on the dashboard. . . . Several times a day he heard a patri-
otic program called 'Lifeline' which praised God, attacked
the United States government, and advertised beans and
corn" (p. 186). The novelist obviously intends the reader
to make a connection between the connotations of beans
and corn and the corny Southern content of the program.
But the association is not regionally fair. Advertisements
of corn and beans and the Jolly Green Giant would not condemn the Tonight Show or a symphony. An author might
ridicule the advertisement but not necessarily the program
sponsored by the advertiser.

The relationship between culture and race is especially apparent in Percy's description of three aunts. As they watch "Strike It Rich," two play canasta, and one reads *Race and Reason* and eats Whitman's Sampler. Although one of them writes love letters to Bill Cullen, they are "good haters, yet not ill-natured . . ." (p. 328). Fearing the book *Race and Reason* will not make clear the connection between race and this shallow, self-indulging, idle culture, Percy deliberately states how these dowagers hate even despite good dispositions.

Southerners eat too much, drink too much, talk too loud, monotonously do the same things over and over, indulge in sexual play, fight too much even in social clubs. Southern culture is grossly physical rather than ideally spiritual. In *The Glass Rooster* a rabidly anti-Negro sheriff is overly physical while an ex-All American football player who is a liberal has de-emphasized the physical in his life. In *The Voice at the Back Door* the county elects a man sheriff because he was an All American football player and a war hero. His coach advises him if he likes music to "keep it to yourself" and to watch out for queers (p. 29).

Even an educated and cultured Southerner is likely to have very poor taste. A physician in *The Numbers of Our Days* marries a poor white who "had been the youngest—and only girl—in a family of eleven children. Her mother had never had the attendance of a doctor at any of the births until Wilma was born" (p. 188). In the late nineteen-twenties or the early thirties the father delivered his own children. The language and manners of this poor girl are so bad that it is hard to believe this sensitive educated physician would marry her. To her brother-in-law she says, "Say, Toam, you must have you a nigger gal somewhere, else you'd not take up for 'em like you do all time" (p. 188).

Fiction written for the sake of a social cause still must be measured by the same standards which are applicable to any art. The best fiction embodies its meaning in concrete characters, images, incidents, symbols, things. It does not put aside the vehicle of art to become a discursive essay on the race question. That these novels are often racist is indicated by the frequency of moral and social preachments. The most rabidly anti-Southern novels such as *Look Away, Look Away, Tiger in the Honeysuckle,* and *Birthright* at times become mere discussions of race problems.

Hostile portraits of the Southern white and Southern culture can have little good effect. They can perhaps assuage novelists' feelings of guilt about their own heritage or make them feel superior to their fellow Southerners. Good fiction, however, is not written by a novelist wishing to pluck the mote out of his own eye. It may move a poor and shallow reader to sympathy for the Negro, but a reader converted by these novels will not have the intelligence to be an effective campaigner for Negro rights. This fiction cannot establish any belief which will make a conservative more liberal. "Good writing," William Empson has written, "is not done unless there are serious forces at work; and it is not permanent unless it works for readers with opinions different from the author's."[37] Southern novels are so permeated with bigoted anti-white propaganda that they cannot work for any reader but those with anti-Southern, pro-black, anti-white hostilities and sympathies. These novels are "not permanent"; they are propaganda. They can only make a white-hater a greater white-hater. A man does not become converted by a novelist who holds him in contempt. These writers may rouse gullible Negroes and Northerners to anger, but surely that cannot be a conscious and honest purpose of the fiction—it is written to condemn anger and hatred. The more racist these novels are, the falser they are. They are guilty of being filled with the same kind of racist hatred which they condemn.

FOUR

Alienated Novelists

A CRITIC OR A NOVELIST CAN DEFEND RACIST FICTION BY pointing to an actual historical or social event which is parallel to an atrocity in fiction. But these novels are stranger than truth: they are not truly justifiable on the basis of fact. As much as a historian, an artist has an obligation to the truth of the heart and of the fact. The artist stands responsible for selection. He must control and limit the extremes of human nature. Taste and common sense help to show when human beings are stereotyped and exaggerated until they are no longer human enough to make good subjects. When the novelist chooses an absurd situation, combines one freak with many others, and associates the freakishness with whites involved in racial turmoil, fiction has been overcome by a social issue.

Bigoted novelists have recently documented in full the evils of the white, but they have seldom represented the accomplishments of Southern whites in their associations with Negroes. Nor do they show any weaknesses in Negroes. Daily harmonious relationships between white and black without a constant thought of racial conflict exist more in fact than in novels. If fact corresponded to fiction, blood let for a racist cause would run almost daily in every Southern village. Black extremists simply do not appear at all in fiction. Negro crime is almost entirely ignored. These novels have no Negro policemen although six Southern cities had Negro police as early as 1942 and by 1952 approximate-

ly one hundred Southern towns had black police.[1] Negro
politicians do not exist in this fiction to represent the
numerous recent successes of Negroes at the polls or the accomplishment of the Negro who served three terms in the
Kentucky legislature before 1942.[2] The reason is obvious:
a successful Negro politician would destroy the racial propaganda of the fiction.

Southern novelists create too few characters like the
"many good people" Charles Evers knows in Mississippi—
even if they "are afraid to speak out."[3] Southern white men,
Mr. Evers says, admire "any man who stands up for what
he believes," but the novelists seldom create a Southerner
of this kind. Negroes in Mississippi, according to Evers,
"are freer than Negroes in Chicago and New York. Because
we know where this [white] man stands. In Chicago and
New York you wonder. They rub you down and they grin in
your face and they stab you in the back. . . . It's one thing
about the Southern white man, in most cases once he says
he'll do something, if you can get him to stand up, once he
commits himself, you can just about trust what he says. Not
in all cases, but in most cases."[4] Surprisingly, Mr. Evers
respects the white more than white novelists respect their
own race. Novels about the race question where the "most"
white men can be trusted could be counted on the fingers
of a hand which had been caught in a circle saw. The fiction
also fails to create many Southern white men who can be
trusted in some ways and not in others. It ignores, in other
words, the vast majority of the white race and makes every
man a saint or a devil.

Ironically the bigotry of the liberal Southern white novelist comes at a time when minorities are more successful
in defense of themselves than ever before. Only the Negro
may joke about Negroes in television or motion pictures.
Racial jokes are in bad taste unless they caricature a Southerner. No people except the Southern whites are pictured

in art as humorous or violent because of race or political persuasion. Many Southern writers fail to defend even the good aspects of their tradition and their heritage.

With a few exceptions, American writers have remained devoted to the geographical places of their origins. New England writers were loyal to New England, sometimes even sanctimoniously and fanatically so. The Old South kept its writers at home before and after the Civil War. Right or wrong, older Southern writers were loyal: "fourteen proslavery novels and one long poem [were] published in the three years (1852–54), following the appearance of Uncle Tom's Cabin."[5] Writers have gone from one extreme to another. In the twentieth century they become displaced authors who live abroad or in the North and who still write about home. William Faulkner and prominent women writers like Ellen Glasgow, Elizabeth Madox Roberts, and Eudora Welty remained in their home communities. But Mark Twain, Thomas Wolfe, and even the most prominent of the Fugitive-Agrarians (except for Donald Davidson) have been lured away to the golden North. One cause of displaced authors is simply the fact that the South has not been an economic center until at least after World War II. Another is that publishers of fiction are almost nonexistent south of Philadelphia. Even Faulkner composed fiction in the offices of his New York publishers. It is difficult to imagine a country of the size and prestige of the United States not having a prominent publisher in the nation's capital when the city is as large as Washington.

Many authors (most notably Carson McCullers and Elizabeth Spencer) have been alienated from the social order of their native region. Perhaps much of the alienation occurs after the author's move to the North. The displaced Southerner writes of the past and his childhood. Sometimes he revisits his native region, but mostly he writes about the South he had known in wonder and love—and hatred too.

Because of distance in time as well as place, the South becomes an oversimplification as the author forgets details of what he had known and fails to touch the earth of youth. "It was very exciting," says Elizabeth Spencer, "to write about the South from the distance of Italy, for the outlines of things stood out very clearly in my mind."[6] Too clearly and too simply. Changes are read about and not observed. These may be some of the reasons for the erroneous facts, the maliciously false history, the fictitious sociology, and some of the most prejudiced literature known to man.

The South, Walter Sullivan has argued, "has suffered the common alienation." Cut off from his rural cultural heritage and from the "ordinary citizen," the Southern writer "frequently . . . eschews Southern society totally and goes to live in a more congenial place such as Roxbury, Connecticut. Finally, the Southern writer or intellectual is as conformist in his ethical and aesthetic dispositions as the artists and intellectuals of New York or California or New Mexico."[7] It is not surprising that the subject in regard to which the writer expresses his alienation most completely is race. The relationship between the white man and the black man, good and bad, has been one distinguishing characteristic of the South. But race is just one factor in the decline of Southern fiction. The simplistic treatment of black and white is symbolic of the novelist's failure to comprehend the complexity of humanity in a racial situation or any other kind.

The damage done to art is greater and more lasting than the social damage done to the South. After all, these novels as social and racial documents will trap only the gullible, will convince only those already seduced by false racial doctrines. The greatest loss is to literature. The poetry of Southern language and the rhetoric of a few decades ago have been turned now into an inferior vehicle of political persuasion. Great Southern characters of the recent past have degenerated into sentimentalized figures sketched for racist aims rather than designed as great literature. Instead of the genuine drama of the past, emotionalized melodrama now provides oversimplified motivations. Type characters are good and bad according to simple black and white racial and moral categories. Melodramatic fiction is written expediently to promote reform, to assuage the conscience which is feeling guilty about racism, and to exploit the literary market. The death of art in the recent Southern novel perhaps was not caused by the subject of race, but the art of fiction has certainly died in novels about race since the Supreme Court decision of 1954.

The pattern is set. Novels on the race question in the future are likely to resemble the fictitious propaganda of old. The techniques, the subject matter, the attitudes—all the ingredients are nearly always the same. The great novels about the struggles between white and black in the modern South remain to be written. If such fiction is ever created, the reader will not be able to tell whether the novelist is a white man or a black man, and possibly the fiction will be neither liberal nor conservative. It will contain members of both races who range the whole breadth of the political spectrum. Black man and white man will love each other despite politics in ways other than the sexual. In other words, any great author who writes about racial struggles anywhere must first write profoundly about the human heart, and all other things will then be added unto him.

Notes

ONE—*Racism in Fiction*

1. "To Whom Is the Poet Responsible?" *Collected Essays* (Denver, 1959), p. 403.
2. This study ignores novels set in the nineteenth century such as Robert Penn Warren's *Wilderness* and William Styron's *The Confessions of Nat Turner*. Slavery, the difference between historical fiction and fiction on a contemporary issue, and the milieu of the time might make the study too difficult if such novels were included. I am also arbitrarily disregarding all short stories purely for the sake of limiting the labor. Novels published before 1954 and after 1968 are not considered. The forty-two Southern novels which I read should be an adequate sampling. In the bibliography I list the thirty-four novels which form the main basis for this study.
3. "The New Provincialism," *Collected Essays*, p. 291.
4. "That Same Pain, That Same Pleasure: An Interview," *Shadow and Act* (New York, 1964), p. 21.
5. "Around Town," *Atlanta Journal*, September 11, 1968.
6. Ralph Ellison, "Twentieth-Century Fiction and the Black Mask of Humanity," *Shadow and Act*, p. 26.
7. "Twentieth-Century Fiction and the Black Mask of Humanity," p. 25.
8. "Negro Character as Seen by White Authors," *Journal of Negro Education*, II (April 1933), p. 179.
9. "Twentieth-Century Fiction and the Black Mask of Humanity," *Shadow and Act*, p. 41.
10. See Francis Irby Gwaltney, *The Numbers of Our Days*.

TWO—*The Black*

1. Ralph Ellison, "Richard Wright's Blues," *Shadow and Act*, p. 83.
2. Ibid., p. 86.
3. "Change the Joke and Slip the Yoke," *Shadow and Act*, p. 48.
4. Robert Frost, "The Ax-Helve," *Complete Poems of Robert Frost* (New York, 1949), p. 229.

5. Ellison, "Twentieth-Century Fiction and the Black Mask of Humanity," *Shadow and Act*, p. 25.

6. *Who Speaks for the Negro?* (New York, 1965), p. 436.

7. Ibid., p. 438.

8. Ibid., pp. 438–439.

9. Others are Elliott Chaze, *Tiger in the Honeysuckle*; Peter S. Feibleman, *A Place Without Twilight*; Mary Beechwood, *Memphis Jackson's Son*; Douglas Kiker, *The Southerner*; Lettie Hamlett Rogers, *Birthright*; Francis Irby Gwaltney, *The Numbers of Our Days*; Norris Lloyd, *A Dream of Mansions*; William Hoffman, *The Trumpet Unblown*; William McIlwain, *The Glass Rooster*; Byron Herbert Reece, *The Hawk and the Sun*.

10. Reynolds Price, *A Long and Happy Life*; Charlotte Payne Johnson, *Watching at the Window*; Walker Percy, *The Last Gentleman*; Robert Penn Warren, *Flood: A Romance of Our Time*.

11. Lettie Hamlett Rogers, *Birthright*, p. 182.

12. Ben Haas, *Look Away, Look Away* (New York, 1964), p. 371.

13. Chaze, *Tiger in the Honeysuckle*, pp. 199–201.

14. Other perfect victims of white violence are Jim in *Birthright*, Tommy and an innocent Negro girl in *The Glass Rooster*, and Beck Dozer's wife, who is raped by a policeman, in *The Voice at the Back Door*.

15. Brainard Cheney, *This Is Adam*, p. 139.

16. Jesse Hill Ford, *The Liberation of Lord Byron Jones*, p. 91.

17. Lucy Daniels, *Caleb, My Son*, p. 18.

18. See also *Tiger in the Honeysuckle*, p. 2; *Memphis Jackson's Son*, p. 3; *The Southerner*, p. 19; *A Dream of Mansions*, p. 40; *Joanna Lord*, p. 72; *This Is Adam*, pp. 1–2; *The Keepers of the House*, pp. 75–6, 117, 216, 227; *The Voice at the Back Door*, pp. 87, 230.

19. John Ehle, *Move Over, Mountain*, p. 16.

20. Beechwood, *Memphis Jackson's Son*, p. 18. And see Hunt, *Joanna Lord*, p. 357.

21. David McCarthy, *Killing at the Big Tree*, pp. 18–19.

22. A check through approximately 520 entries in Ethel L. Williams, *Biographical Directory of Negro Ministers* (New York, 1965), turned up no Negro pastor in the South with a Ph.D. Fiction contradicts probability here if not fact. Professors and deans in theology schools who are also pastors are not prototypes for this character.

23. Irene C. Edmonds, "Faulkner and the Black Shadow," in *Southern Renascence: The Literature of the Modern South*, ed. Louis D. Rubin, Jr., and Robert D. Jacobs (Baltimore, 1953), pp. 194, 199.

24. Harold P. Marley, "The Negro in Recent Southern Literature," *South Atlantic Quarterly*, XXVII (January 1928), 29.

25. Curiously, the novel most like Feibleman's in portraying the mind of a sensitive Negro female is written by his stepmother, Shirley Ann Grau, in *The Keepers of the House*.

THREE—*The White*

1. Mr. McGill told me this at a luncheon for Robert Penn Warren in 1968.
2. Introduction, *The Voice at the Back Door*, p. xx.
3. *Look Away, Look Away*, p. 331. This statement is made by an admirable character who gives his life for the cause of Negro rights. He commits no wrongs. His views are supported by the theme of the entire novel. It seems safe to assume therefore that the character and the novelist agree.
4. *The Southerner*, p. 34.
5. Harry A. Ploski and Roscoe C. Brown, Jr., *The Negro Almanac* (New York, 1967), p. 214.
6. *A Place for My Head*, p. 223.
7. Gwaltney, *The Numbers of Our Days*, p. 23.
8. Ibid., p. 121.
9. Ibid., p. 173.
10. Ibid., pp. 174–175.
11. McCullers, *Clock Without Hands*, p. 22.
12. Lee, *To Kill a Mockingbird*, p. 97.
13. Hunt, *Joanna Lord*, p. 91.
14. McIlwain, *The Glass Rooster*, p. 214.
15. Ford, *The Liberation of Lord Byron Jones*, p. 33.
16. "Literary Horizons," *Saturday Review*, LII (February 8, 1969), 22.
17. New York, 1964, p. 44.
18. Gwaltney, *The Numbers of Our Days*, p. 263.
19. McIlwain, *The Glass Rooster*, p. 54; see also Grau, *The Keepers of the House*, p. 215; Faulkner, *The Reivers*, p. 172; Francis Gwaltney, *The Yeller-Headed Summer* (New York, 1954), p. 7.
20. Pages 111–112. See also Daniels, *Caleb, My Son*, p. 16; Feibleman, *A Place Without Twilight*, p. 83.
21. See Reece, *The Hawk and the Sun*, pp. 142–143; Lloyd, *A Dream of Mansions*, pp. 223, 263; Kiker, *The Southerner*, p. 72.
22. I have compiled these statistics with some care, but they must be considered representative rather than precise. Murders which are merely alluded to, for example, are omitted. If I counted the crimes again, I could not arrive at the same numbers, but the conclusions would add up to similar results.
23. *Uniform Crime Reports for the United States—1965* (Washington, 1966), p. 117.
24. McIlwain, *The Glass Rooster*, p. 234; Lee, *To Kill a Mockingbird*, pp. 184, 206. See also Kiker, *The Southerner*, p. 209.
25. See Chaze, *Tiger in the Honeysuckle*, p. 260.
26. Hoffman, *A Place for My Head*, p. 64.
27. Rogers, *Birthright*, p. 37.

28. Pages 315–316.
29. Cheney, *This Is Adam*, p. 266.
30. Norris, *All the Kingdoms of Earth*, p. 66.
31. Daniels, *Caleb, My Son*, p. 97.
32. See also *Move Over, Mountain*, p. 144.
33. *The Daughters of Necessity* (Cleveland, 1959), p. 9.
34. New York, 1958, p. 3.
35. See also Montgomery, *The Wandering of Desire*, p. 9; Lee, *To Kill a Mockingbird*, p. 11.
36. McIlwain, *The Glass Rooster*, p. 186.
37. *English Pastoral Poetry* (New York, 1938), p. 3.

FOUR—*Alienated Novelists*

1. Virginius Dabney, *Below the Potomac: A Book about the New South* (New York, 1942), p. 194; Hodding Carter, *Where Main Street Meets the River* (New York, 1953), p. 243.
2. Dabney, pp. 198–199.
3. Warren, *Who Speaks for the Negro?*, p. 104.
4. Ibid., p. 107.
5. Jeannette Reid Tandy, "Pro-Slavery Propaganda in American Fiction of the Fifties," *South Atlantic Quarterly*, XXI (January 1922), 41.
6. Introduction, *The Voice at the Back Door*, p. xviii.
7. "The New Faustus: The Southern Renascence and the Joycean Aesthetic," in *Southern Fiction Today: Renascence and Beyond*, ed. George Core (Athens, 1969), pp. 12–13.

Bibliography

The following novels written by Southern white authors between 1954 and 1968 treat racial relations in the modern South. Negro characters and racial conflict play minor roles in a few of these but are significant in the overwhelming majority. I have used these novels as the basis for *The Death of Art.*

Beechwood, Mary. *Memphis Jackson's Son.* Boston: Houghton Mifflin, 1956.

Blythe, LeGette. *Call Down the Storm.* New York: Holt, 1958.

Chaze, Elliott. *Tiger in the Honeysuckle.* New York: Charles Scribner's Sons, 1965.

Cheney, Brainard. *This Is Adam.* New York: McDowell, Obolensky, 1958.

Daniels, Lucy. *Caleb, My Son.* Philadelphia: J. B. Lippincott, 1956.

Davis, Paxton. *The Seasons of Heroes.* New York: William Morrow, 1967.

Ehle, John. *Move Over, Mountain.* New York: William Morrow, 1957.

Faulkner, William. *The Reivers: A Reminiscence.* New York: Random House, 1962.

Feibleman, Peter S. *A Place Without Twilight.* Cleveland: World Publishing Company, 1958.

Ford, Jesse Hill. *The Liberation of Lord Byron Jones.* Boston: Little, Brown, 1965.

Grau, Shirley Ann. *The Keepers of the House.* New York: Alfred A. Knopf, 1964.

Gwaltney, Francis Irby. *The Numbers of Our Days.* New York: Random House, 1959.

————. *A Step in the River.* New York: Random House, 1960.

Haas, Ben. *Look Away, Look Away.* New York: Simon and Schuster, 1964.

Hoffman, William. *A Place for My Head.* Garden City: Doubleday, 1960.

————. *The Trumpet Unblown.* Garden City: Doubleday, 1955.

Hunt, Mary Fassett. *Joanna Lord.* Indianapolis: Bobbs-Merrill, 1954.

Johnson, Charlotte Payne. *Watching at the Window.* Indianapolis: Bobbs-Merrill, 1955.

Kiker, Douglas. *The Southerner.* New York: Rinehart, 1957.

Lee, Harper. *To Kill a Mockingbird.* Philadelphia: J. B. Lippincott, 1960.

Lloyd, Norris. *A Dream of Mansions.* New York: Random House, 1962.

McCarthy, David. *Killing at the Big Tree.* Garden City: Doubleday, 1960.

McCullers, Carson. *Clock Without Hands.* Boston: Houghton Mifflin, 1961.

McIlwain, William. *The Glass Rooster.* Garden City: Doubleday, 1960.

Montgomery, Marion. *The Wandering of Desire.* New York: Harper, 1962.

Norris, Hoke. *All the Kingdoms of Earth.* New York: Simon and Schuster, 1956.

Percy, Walker. *The Last Gentleman.* New York: Farrar, Straus and Giroux, 1966.

Price, Reynolds. *A Long and Happy Life.* New York: Atheneum, 1962.

Reece, Byron Herbert. *The Hawk and the Sun.* New York: E. P. Dutton, 1955.

Rogers, Lettie Hamlett. *Birthright.* New York: Simon and Schuster, 1957.

Smith, Lillian. *One Hour.* New York: Harcourt, Brace, 1959.

Spencer, Elizabeth. *The Voice at the Back Door.* New York: McGraw-Hill Book Company, 1956. Also published, with an introduction by the author, in a Time Reading Program Special Edition (New York, 1965). The latter edition is the one cited in this study.

Styron, William. *Set This House on Fire.* New York: Random House, 1960.

Warren, Robert Penn. *Flood: A Romance of Our Time.* New York: Random House, 1964.

Index

The only items referred to in the index are authors and books, with books appearing under the author's name. Some books and authors not in the bibliography appear in the index.

Beechwood, Mary: *Memphis Jackson's Son*, 6–7, 24–25
Blythe, LeGette: *Call Down the Storm*, 15
Brown, Sterling A., 4, 27

Chaze, Elliott: *Tiger in the Honeysuckle*, 7–8, 20, 29, 43–44, 56–57, 60
Cheney, Brainard: *This Is Adam*, 14, 22, 25, 52–53

Daniels, Lucy: *Caleb, My Son*, 15, 16, 22, 54
Davidson, Donald, 63
Davis, Paxton: *The Seasons of Heroes*, 15

Edmonds, Irene C., 25–26
Empson, William, 60
Ehle, John: *Move Over, Mountain*, 15, 23, 54–55
Ellison, Ralph: 2, 4–5, 11–12, 38

Faulkner, William: 53, 63; *Absalom, Absalom!*, 1; *As I Lay Dying*, 3; *The Reivers: A Reminiscence*, 9, 14, 25, 28, 44, 57
Feibleman, Peter S.: *The Daughters of Necessity*, 57; *A Place Without Twilight*, 17, 26–27, 28, 33, 52
Ford, Jesse Hill: *The Liberation of Lord Byron Jones*, 6, 14, 19, 21–22, 29–30, 32–33, 39–42, 51, 55

Glasgow, Ellen, 63
Grau, Shirley Ann: *The Keepers of the House*, 14, 20
Greene, Graham, 4

Gwaltney, Francis Irby: *The Numbers of Our Days*, 18, 20–21, 25, 28, 38, 51, 59; *The Yeller-Headed Summer*, 44

Haas, Ben: *Look Away, Look Away*, 5, 14, 19–20, 21, 30, 32, 36, 42, 46, 49–50, 52, 54, 60
Harte, Bret, 17
Heyward, DuBose, 26
Hicks, Granville, 42
Hoffman, William: *A Place for My Head*, 15, 25, 38, 51, 54, 57–58; *The Trumpet Unblown*, 8, 28
Humphrey, William: *Home from the Hill*, 57
Hunt, Mary Fassett: *Joanna Lord*, 3, 14, 15–16, 24, 31, 37, 39

Johnson, Charlotte Payne: *Watching at the Window*, 16–17, 28, 44
Jones, Madison: *An Exile*, 45–46

Kiker, Douglas: *The Southerner*, 7, 29, 31, 32, 36–37, 53–54

Lee, Harper, *To Kill a Mockingbird*: 6, 9, 14, 22–23, 23–24, 28, 35, 38–39, 44
Lloyd, Norris: *A Dream of Mansions*, 18, 28
Lewis, Sinclair, 53

McCarthy, David; *Killing at the Big Tree*, 14, 31, 44–45
McCullers, Carson: 35, 63; *Clock Without Hands*, 14, 21, 25, 29, 44, 50, 52, 55–56, 57
McGill, Ralph, 35, 42
McIlwain, William: *The Glass Rooster*, 15, 42, 59
Montgomery, Marion: *The Wandering of Desire*, 15
Murfree, Mary Noailles, 3, 17

Norris, Hoke: *All the Kingdoms of Earth*, 15, 17–18, 20, 54

Park, Hugh, 3
Patterson, Eugene, 42
Percy, Walker: *The Last Gentleman*, 28, 37–38, 47, 58–59
Peterkin, Julia, 26
Price, Reynolds: *A Long and Happy Life*, 3, 28

Reece, Byron Herbert: *The Hawk and the Sun*, 20, 21, 28
Roberts, Elizabeth Madox, 63
Rogers, Lettie Hamlett: *Birthright*, 28, 50, 51–52, 60

Smith, Lillian: 42–43; *One Hour*, 52
Spencer, Elizabeth: 63, 64; *The Voice at the Back Door*, 14, 17, 18–19, 20, 25, 28, 35–36, 44–45, 50, 57, 59
Stowe, Harriet Beecher: *Uncle Tom's Cabin*, 63
Styron, William: *The Confessions of Nat Turner*, 67n; *Set This House on Fire*, 8–9, 14, 38, 57
Sullivan, Walter, 64

Tate, Allen, 1, 2
Twain, Mark, 63

Warren, Robert Penn: 4, 12–13, 42, 53; *Flood*, 9, 20, 25, 32, 45–46; *Wilderness*, 67n
Welty, Eudora: 53, 63
Wolfe, Thomas: 53, 63; *Look Homeward, Angel*, 52